KALAHARI
Wild Africa

LORENZ A. FISCHER · JUDITH BURRI

KALAHARI
Wild Africa

B BUCHER

Two black stripes run down the cheetah's face like tears. According to the legend, they are crying over their lost children, as of the five cubs in a litter a female cheetah usually only manages to raise one or two.

KALAHARI -Wild Africa

"With regard to the number of large quadrupeds, there certainly exists no quarter of the globe which will bear comparison with Southern Africa."

CHARLES DARWIN
BRITISH NATURALIST (1809–1955)
IN:
"THE VOYAGE OF THE BEAGLE", 1939

A young elephant, experiences the luxury of rubbing itself against a tree to get rid of skin parasites.

PREFACE

TEN YEARS AGO, WE TRAVELED TO BOTSWANA FOR THE FIRST TIME – right into the middle of the Kalahari. Equipped with an off-road vehicle and supplies of water, fuel and food we drove through unspoilt regions, devoid of human beings, for days on end. We were fascinated, discovering a new world, a world still dominated by animals. In the evenings, we would sit by our campfire, listening to the strange sounds, which – with time – we managed to interpret. We spent our days at the water holes where the African animals came together to drink, always following the same life-rhythm. Full of awe we watched the large elephant and buffalo herds at the Chobe, the rare wild dogs in the Moremi Reserve and the hunting lions and took photos of them.

Our passion for the wild, untamed Africa led us back to the Kalahari, time and time again. Meanwhile we have spent more than a year in the national parks of Botswana, Namibia and South Africa. During our last trips, we focused on working on this book for six months while simultaneously developing a multi-vision presentation.

This book is divided into three parts that correspond to the main habitats of the Kalahari: the savannah, the saltpans and the rivers, which we have assigned the Okavango Delta to as well. Each one of these three chapters contains stories experienced and researched by us. They are stories of encounters with wild animals, with unspoilt landscapes and with people whose ancestors have lived in the Kalahari since the Stone Age. With our photographs, allow us to whisk you far away from civilization to this awe-inspiring place, a natural paradise.

THE KALAHARI
THE WORLD'S LARGEST AREA OF SAND

AN ENDLESS EXPANSE OF GOLDEN SAVANNA. Herds of antelope and zebras grazing and migrating across the plain, making the best of the cool morning temperatures. A family of meerkats is standing in the sun sleepily, only just beginning to warm up. Two cheetahs, searching for a shady spot in the dried out riverbed and somewhere to lie down in order to rest after an unsuccessful hunt. An Oryx antelope standing still on a red sand dune, hoping to get some relief from the midday heat by the rising wind. Elephants, chasing away a thirsty jackal from the waterhole against the backdrop of a magnificent sunset. A clear, starry night, the mighty roars of lions and the eerie squeals of laughter from hyenas fighting over their prey, disrupt the silence. This is the Kalahari, the Africa of our dreams, or in Nelson Mandela's words: the Africa of myths and legends.

The Kalahari is a gigantic basin in Southern Africa, filled with sand. It stretches from the North of South Africa over Botswana and the East of Namibia to Zimbabwe, Zambia, Angola into the Congo. With over one million square kilometers (362500 square miles), it is three times bigger than Germany! Astonishingly however, the biggest coherent area of sand in the world is by no means a desert. Depending on precipitation and the water table, grass, bushes and even trees are growing on the sandy soil.

Nevertheless, conditions are tough for humans, plants and animals. The temperature fluctuations are extreme. In the summer, the temperatures rise to over 40 degrees Celsius, in winter they can drop to minus 10 degrees Celsius. The sparse rains during the wet season seep away quickly. In this barren place, surface water is only temporarily available. There are almost no lakes and rivers. Consequently, evolving amazing techniques to adapt to the arid climate and the constant quest for water is the driving force behind life in the Kalahari; but wherever you do find water, you encounter a breathtaking diversity of African animals.

In the Kalahari, water has also created some of the most fascinating landscapes on our planet. During the wet season, 100,000 birds from all over Africa breed around the largest dried up salt lake in the world, the Makgadikgadi Pans. At the Victoria Falls, the largest waterfall in Africa, the Zambezi crashes into a canyon over 100 meters (328 feet) deep along a length of almost two kilometers (1.25 miles). The swamp area of the

Okavango Delta is one of the most species rich and diverse natural wonders on Earth. UNESCO declared the Victoria Falls as World Heritage for humankind. The Okavango delta is a wetland of international importance according to the RAMSAR Convention.

For thousands of years the only inhabitants of Kalahari were bush people, a people of hunters and gatherers. Black pastoral people and the white cattle breeders, who arrived later, stayed close to the rivers. Only in the last century after the groundwater could be tapped via boreholes, did they venture into central Kalahari. Even so, its population density remains low to this day, as the sparse land has little to offer. Large areas of the Kalahari remain unpopulated. In these areas, where there is no human impact, the original African wilderness remains conserved.

Oryx antelopes have adapted perfectly to very dry habitats such as those of the Central Kalahari Game Reserve in Botswana. They do not need any water and only start to sweat when their bodies reach a dangerously high temperature. Certainly, their body temperature can rise up to 45 degrees Celsius. A complicated network of blood vessels in their nasal area cools their blood down to an agreeable 40 °C, before it reaches the sensitive brain.

PAGE 18/19 During the dry season, elephant bulls occupy the water holes of Savuti in Chobe National Park, Botswana.

THE SAVANNAS

THERE HAS NOT BEEN A DROP OF RAIN IN MONTHS. Life in the African savanna is defined by the search for food and water. The last remaining waterholes are crowded; there is a permanent coming and going. Many animals cover long distances every day, migrating between the water holes and the areas where they feed. Their feeding habits vary. Wildebeest and zebras graze in small groups, nibbling the short golden grass. Antelopes, giraffes and elephants pick the last dry leaves off the trees and the predators – the lions, hyenas, leopards, cheetahs and wild dogs go for the weakened animals of prey.

In October, the humidity starts to build up in the cloudy sky. The heat becomes almost unbearable. Both animals and humans limit their activities to the absolute minimum. Tight groups of animals gather under every bush, seeking the sparse shadow. Then – finally – a violent storm brings relief at last! Heavy rains cool down the parched land. Nature regains new life. After just a few days, green shoots cover the sandy ground. Bullfrogs emerge miraculously, digging themselves out of the clay that was rock hard only moments before. Termites swarm out in huge numbers to found a new colony and elephants and antelopes return to previously deserted areas, where food and water has now become available in abundance. This dramatic change between dry and wet periods is typical for the savanna.

There is no other place on Earth with such a wide diversity of large mammals. For us, as human beings, the African savanna evokes a feeling of freedom in a wilderness and a sense of adventure! Gazing over the wide-open grassland, we journey back in time to millions of years ago when our ancestors struggled to survive here. Today, by European standards, the natural wildlife flourishes in the huge protected areas.

After months of drought, the first rains in October have refilled the clay pans in Chobe National Park with water.

TOP *When the meerkats of southern Kalahari dig for insects or scorpions, one of them always keeps watch and carefully surveys the area. With their incredibly sharp eyesight, they can distinguish a dangerous bird of prey from a harmless vulture from a distance of two kilometers away. When danger threatens, they flee into their earth holes, which are scattered all over their territory.*
RIGHT *In the Kgalagadi Transfrontier Park, a springbok stirs up the mud with its hoofs. In doing so, it enriches the water he laps up with valuable soil minerals.*

PAGE 24/25 *In the Chobe National Park in Botswana there are more elephants than anywhere else in Africa. During the dry season therefore, there is intense activity both day and night at the water holes of Savuti.*

GENTLE GIANTS
MOVING WITH THE ELEPHANTS

A SICKLY STENCH FILLS THE AIR. Vultures squabble over the mountains of rotting meat. With wings spread out wide, newcomers hop into the thick of it. One by one, they disappear into the belly of the carcass, greedy for a tasty morsel. With determination a hyena rips a new hole through the tough elephant hide and pulls out a large piece of meat from the carcass, its face covered in blood.

We spend several hours near the dead elephant bull. He died a few days ago from old age here on the bank of a water hole in Savuti. His death has troubled the other elephants. They hardly have the courage to approach the waterhole to drink. Therefore, the park rangers decide to drag the carcass several hundred meters away. Eventually the elephants calm down again and manage to accept the death of their friend. A couple of elephant bulls visit him on their way back from the waterhole into the bush. First they chase away the vultures and hyenas. Then they touch the dead elephant gently all over with their sensitive trunks. After half an hour of grieving they leave the carcass to the carrion feeders again.

Elephants form complex social relationships and display feelings including mourning, joy, love and jealousy. Recently scientists discovered that elephants recognize their mirror image and must therefore have a kind of self-awareness. Apart from us humans, until now this was only attributed to large apes and dolphins. Equally fascinating is the fact that Elephants communicate with each other through a rich and varied language. Up until now, 70 different sounds have been identified. The human ear can only detect these deep tones in the infrasound range with technical aids. Elephants use these lower frequencies to communicate over distances of many kilometers. Incidentally, female elephants talk to each other much more than the males do.

Mature elephant bulls lead a solitary life, but enjoy loose friendships with other bulls. In the dry season, many of the mighty old bulls of the Chobe National Park are found in Savuti. Each day they migrate to one of the few waterholes to drink. If the waterhole appears occupied, strength and body size determine who is allowed to call the waterhole his own. Sometimes smaller elephants are put in their places by a firm shove against their behinds.

In the early morning hours, the mighty elephants share the water hole with lots of thirsty Namaqua Doves.

TOP ROW *When an elephant dies, hyenas, vultures and lions have a rich feed. Vultures are usually the first to arrive at the scene. The hyenas watch the flight of the birds and follow them. Hyenas have the strongest set of jaws in the entire animal kingdom. They can crack open even the biggest bones. Very soon, all that is left of the grey colossus is its skull and a few large bones.*

BOTTOM LEFT *An elephant herd shows distress when, on its way to the waterhole, it comes across the carcass of a bull which has recently died. Elephants grieve over their deads. They are particularly affected by the death of a family member. When a family member dies, they often stay with the carcass for days, as if they were giving a good-bye ritual.*

BOTTOM RIGHT *The elephants only start coming to the water hole again after the park rangers have dragged the dead animal a few hundred meters (feet) away.*

Elephants drink at least 70 to 90 liters (18.5 to 25 US-gallons) a day. If they are very thirsty, they can drink as much as 150 liters (approx. 40 US-gallons). A warthog also tries to get to the water amongst the throng of giants. On the back of the elephants, Oxpeckers feed on fleas, mites and ticks.

TOP LEFT *After they have drunk their fill, elephants devote their attention to body care – they squirt water and mud over themselves. The little ones are still a little clumsy with this.*

TOP RIGHT *Elephant babies find safety and shade under their mother's belly.*

BOTTOM LEFT *Although the elephant's skin is up to three centimeters (1.2 inches) thick in places, it is still highly sensitive. An elephant feels every fly landing on it.*

BOTTOM RIGHT *An elephant family avoids the midday heat by huddling up close in the shade. Elephants do not sweat, but give off heat over their large ears, which are well supplied with blood.*

The elephants of Botswana are the largest in the world. The bulls grow up to a height of four meters (13 feet) and can weigh up to seven tonnes. Their tusks, however, are smaller than those of the elephants in Kenya are. As in the Kalahari, their food contains only few minerals so their tusks wear down faster.

We never ceased to be amazed at how silently these giants, weighing up to seven tons, can move. A fatty pad of tissue between the foot and the sole dampens their steps. Frequently we only became aware of an elephant when it was almost standing right next to us!

The old elephant bulls in Botswana are very peaceful. With several years of life's experiences, an old elephant hardly ever loses its cool. However, during the musth, a kind of rut, testosterone changes him into an aggressive roughneck. On his search for a fertile elephant cow, he leaves drops of urine behind, forming a pungently smelling trace. Temporin, an olfactory signal, oozes from his temporal glands, signalizing his condition

to other elephants, which quickly get out of his way. Only another hormone-ridden musth bull would dare measure his strength with him in this state. Bulls have serious fights over elephant cows. Only the winners get the chance to mate.

We leave the elephant bulls in Savuti and drive north to the Chobe River. In the dry season hundreds of elephant families assemble here. Lead by an experienced cow, the families consist of sisters and daughters who all look after the calves together. In the early morning we find them in the bush, calmly grazing on grass and foliage. They adeptly rotate individual twigs in their mouths until all the bark has been rasped off. To reach the leaves in the crown of the trees, they do not hesitate to push over the entire tree. An

At the water hole, the strongest is served first. The largest elephant occupies the best spot. Equally, large elephants measure their strength by pressing their heads against each other. Only elephants in musth, a kind of rut, start serious fights. Temporarily, they are extremely aggressive, thus, even driving away larger rivals.

elephant devours up to 200 kilograms of plant material every day. Thus, the hinterland of Chobe looks pretty ravaged towards the end of the dry season. In the north of Botswana there are approximately 120,000 elephants, more than anywhere else on Earth. Therefore the population spread to the neighboring countries Namibia, Angola, Zimbabwe und Zambia.

Just like the elephant families, we also avoid the midday heat by resting in the shadow of a tree. When it cools down a little in the afternoon, we drive to the river. This is when the elephants move to the water, too. Elephant families greet each other joyfully by putting their trunk into each other's mouth and by sniffing at each other's temporal glands. After having drunk to the full, they devote themselves to body care. To protect their sensitive skin from the sun and from parasites they squirt mud over each other with their trunks, some of them role around in it with relish, others find a more quiet spot for a proper bath, with only their trunk emerging out of the water like a snorkel. The daily ritual ends with a dust bath.

The little elephant calves frolic around playfully between the huge bodies. Their mothers nurture them, but their aunts and older sisters protect and raise them, too. They explore the world with boundless joy of life and are up to all sorts of mischief. One of the little ones, for instance, chases a warthog, trumpeting loudly; but the very tiniest elephant forms the center of attention. His pink ears are proof that he can only be a few days old. His trunk dangles around aimlessly while he walks and he immediately trips over even the slightest obstacle, instigating hectic attention amongst the cows. From all sides the mature cows hurry to help him up on his feet again. They have all partaken in his birth around a week ago. A birth, just like a death, is a special event in the life of an elephant, an event which is shared by the whole family.

Elephant bulls are loners. Befriended bulls only
move around temporarily in small groups.
Frequently an old bull will look after a young one
who has just left his family.

"I dream of the realization of the unity of Africa, whereby its leaders combine in their efforts to solve the problems of this continent. I dream of our vast deserts, of our forests, of all our great wildernesses."

NELSON MANDELA,
SOUTH AFRICAN STATESMAN,
FIRST DEMOCRATICALLY ELECTED STATE
PRESIDENT OF SOUTH AFRICA IN 1994,
NOBEL PRIZE FOR PEACE IN 1993
(BORN 1918)

LEFT *During the dry season thousands of zebras in Makgadikgadi National Park migrate daily from their pastures to the water holes at the Boteti River.*
TOP *Zebras are nervous and edgy at the water hole for fear of lions. Repeatedly they gallop off in response to a false alarm, only to return to the water hole shortly afterwards.*

PAGE 36/37 *Lead by the dominant cows, dozens of elephant families wander to the Chobe River towards the evening.*

TOP ROW *The Ground Hornbill (left) picks around for insects, lizards and snakes. The Bateleur eagle (center) is known for its acrobatic flights with rapid changes in direction, nosedives and death defying leaps! They spend almost all day in the air. After having enjoyed a bloody meal the Lappet-faced Vulture (right) takes a bath in a water hole in Kgalagadi Transfrontier Park.*
BOTTOM LEFT *In the dry season, when many trees and bushes have lost their leaves, seeds and fruit are a welcome meal for the large Kudu bull.*
BOTTOM RIGHT *Warthogs feed on grass and dig for roots and small invertebrates. They use their strange long, flat head as a lever.*

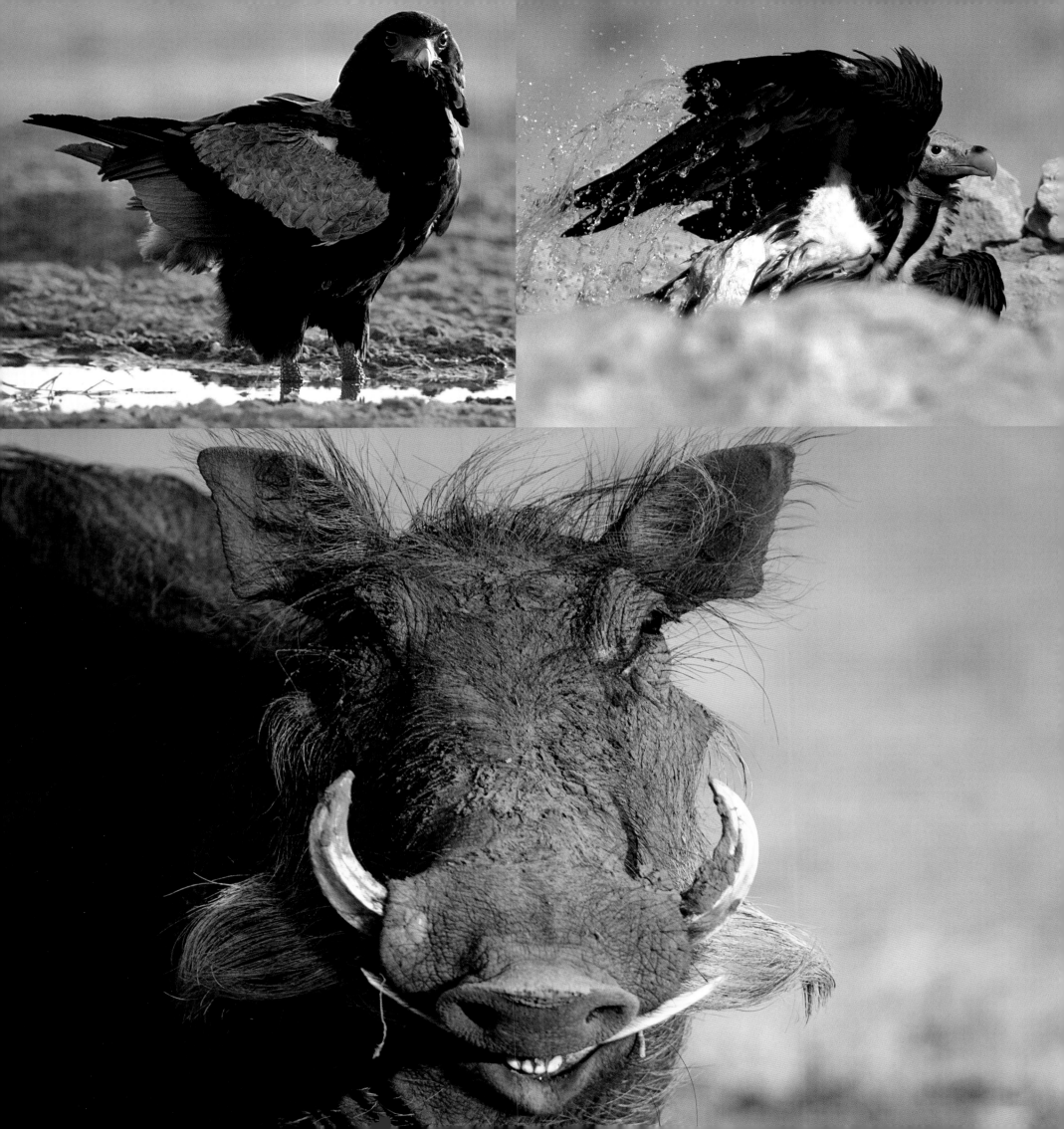

TOP *Like many animals who have adapted to the drought, the elands can survive without water. They graze by night when the plants have higher water content, having absorbed humidity from the air once it has cooled down.*

RIGHT *Blue Wildebeest need to drink regularly. During the dry season, they migrate to holes and rivers, which hold water throughout the year. As soon as it rains, they migrate to the freshly sprouting green grass.*

PAGE 44/45 *Jackals quarrelling at the Savuti water hole in the Chobe National Park. The elephant bull lifts its trunk to be able to pick up scents better.*

THE STONE AGE AND MODERN TIMES
BUSHMEN, THE INDIGENOUS PEOPLE OF SOUTHERN AFRICA

TJOU, BESSA AND THE BOYS, Thomas and /Khi-/Khao ("/" is a clicking sound), sit around the evening fire in front of their grass hut. Their only piece of clothing is a well-used loincloth made of springbok leather. Tjou stuffs a little tobacco into the cocoon of an insect, lights it in the fire and sits back, enjoying his smoke. Bessa tells the boys about their hunting experiences. Fascinated by their melodious language with the strange clicking sounds, we try to get the gist of their story.

Because of these "animal-like sounds", in the 17th century the European colonialists considered the Bushmen to be savages. The anthropologists of the 19th century were even convinced that in them they had found the missing link between apes and humans. Today the Europeans admire the Bushmen because they are the last survivors of a dying culture and continue to live in peace and harmony with nature.

Next day we meet Thomas who is wearing a pair of jeans, a leather coat, sunglasses and a cool red hat. His mother teasingly calls him a gangster. The families of Tjou and Bessa live in employee accommodation at the "Intu Afrika" Lodge. They take tourists into the bush on so-called Bushman Walks to offer them a glimpse of their traditional ways of life.

The Bushmen are the indigenous people of the southern Africa. Rock engravings and paintings up to 27,000 years old document their past. Their language is one of the oldest in the world. As nomadic hunters and gatherers, they populated the Kalahari for over thousands of years. Each year they crossed distances of more than 2,500 kilometers (1,552 miles) on foot in their search for food and water. Their knowledge of the animals and plants of the Kalahari is impressive, their reputation as masters of track reading remains legendary to this day. In the absence of chiefs or kings, problems were discussed amongst the men and women of the whole tribe and everyone had an equal say in making decisions.

Today there are around 100,000 Bushmen in the southern Africa. A third of them live in Namibia, where they belong to the poorest and least respected population sector. Without land rights many of them make their living as cheap farm workers or else they survive on social support, living on the edge of larger settlements. More than 60 per cent

The Bushmen are the indigenous people of the southern Africa. Up to just a few years ago, they roamed through the Kalahari as hunters and gatherers.

When hunting, the Bushmen approach their prey up to a distance of 30 meters (98 feet). From there they shoot a poison arrow. Because the poison takes time to exert its effect, they only start looking for the wounded animal the next day. They follow its tracks until they find the animal, which has usually broken down with exhaustion, but is still alive. They relieve it from its suffering with the thrust of a spear.

of them can neither read nor write and many are unemployed. In our modern world their traditional skills are no longer required.

Whilst the lack of school education excludes the Bushmen from the modern world, their lack of access to the land and its resources prevents them from pursuing their traditional way of life. We drive to the Nyae Nyae Conservancy, on our quest to see tradition and modern times coexisting side by side. In Tsumkwe we meet N/iaci. He is the son of the village elder of Makuri and works as a translator. The five families living in Makuri belong to the 2,500 Ju/íhoan who migrated through the region just a few decades ago. Meanwhile they have settled down. Their children go to the local school. They are the only Bushmen in Namibia who have the land right which allows them to utilize the available resources by hunting and gathering. However, due to their sessile way of life,

the distances they need to cover to find food become longer and longer. In the dry season, there are only few edible plants, berries and fruit and little game in the surrounds of the village. They can therefore only obtain part of their food through hunting and gathering alone.

In order to earn some money, the people of Makuri invite tourists to participate in their traditional activities. In contrast to many lodges, where the tourists have a show presented to them, here in Makuri they experience real everyday bushman life. We observe Tasa digging out a water-containing root with her stick, which we drink there and then to quench our thirst, and then we listen to the men's reports of their last hunting trip to the saltpan, where they hid in earth holes, waiting for kudu antelopes, which they killed with poisoned arrows. We begin to feel as though we have been beamed into a different time!

The meat is shared amongst the entire group. The killed animal does not necessarily belong to the person who has hit it with his arrow; it often belongs to the owner of the arrow. Of course, this does not need to be one and the same person. Bushmen nurture their friendships by giving gifts to each other – aside from his own, every hunter carries arrows of other hunters in his quiver.

The "ntu Africa" lodge near Marienthal in Namibia employs Bushmen to take tourists on walks through the bush. The aim of these bush walks is to show them their former way of life as hunters and gatherers. They no longer live in traditional grass huts, but in lodgings made of brick, in common with all the other employees of the lodge. After work, they take off their leather capes and change into modern clothes.

TOP LEFT *The children of the Bushmen in "Intu Africa" grow up carefree. Bushmen raise their children in an anti-authoritarian manner and treat them with a lot of love and tenderness.*
BOTTOM LEFT *Music and song is an everyday experience for the bush people. Bessa plays the guitar in his free time.*

TOP RIGHT *The baby crying discontentedly amuses the family; but it will not take long before someone tends to it.*
BOTTOM RIGHT *I'Khaitieb enjoys his lunch break with his family. He is particularly proud of his little son.*

The two most experienced old men of the village are responsible for preparing the poisoned arrows. They lead us to one of the few places where the larva of the Diamphidia leaf beetle is to be found. A nerve poison is extracted from this beetle. It takes them more than an hour to dig out seven beetle larvae. Back in the village the larvae are mashed up and mixed with a little plant juice and saliva. Then the old men carefully apply this poisonous mixture to a newly made arrow, just behind its head. They seem to enjoy the work a lot, reveling in memories of past times when they were hunters themselves. The effect of the poison is slow, but lethal. A large antelope takes two or three days to die. Therefore, the hunters return to the village after they have shot an animal with their arrow. Only on the next day do they start following the track of the wounded animal.

We spend the evening with the family of N/iaci, huddled around the fire in front of their hut. News of the day is exchanged over a cup of tea. There is a lot of laughter. When night falls, the women settle around a large fire in the middle of the village. Clapping their hands rhythmically, they start to sing. Their singing, which sounds a little monotonous to us, certainly seems to exert a hypnotic effect on the men. With short stamping steps they close in on the women, ready to dance around them. The dancers keep on improvising new figures. 70-year old Kaece emerges as a passionate dancer, too. Albeit not as flexible as the younger men, he still joins the dance, supported by his stick. "The songs do not have any words," N/iaci explains. "The dances are named by the rain, the sun, the giraffe or other significant things." Then finally even the rather serious and reserved N/iaci gets whirled away by the power of the dance.

TOP *The village elder Kaqece IKaece (right) and his old friend of the same name, Kaqece Iui (left), are the oldest men in the village of Makuri. They are the ones who produce the poison arrows.*
BELOW *To avoid any accidents, care is taken not to cover the tip of the arrow with poison from the leaf beetle. The hunter could scratch his skin, incurring lethal consequences.*

TOP *The Bushmen of Makuri love to sing and dance. Singing and clapping, Tasa Boo and the other women set the beat for the dance.*
RIGHT *The men dance around the women in a circle. Ikaece Kaqece, the eldest son of the village elder, leads the group of men.*

LEFT *The Bushmen refer to the granite Tsodilo Hills as male, female and child. The summit of the male, the highest in Botswana, is only 410 meters (1,345 feet) high. 4,500 rock paintings and numerous archaeological findings bear testimony to human activities 100,000 years ago. In 2001, the Tsodilo Hills were declared world heritage by UNESCO.*
TOP *Ancestors of the Bushmen made the rock paintings. It is thought that shamans, to illustrate what they were experiencing in their trances, did them.*

PAGE 56/57 *The ancestors of today's bush people also made the rock carvings of Twyfelfontein in Namibia.*

The mottled markings of lion cubs usually disappear within the first year. But, with the fair lionesses of the southern Kalahari, these markings remain visible on their legs. Mothers and aunts raise the cubs jointly. Often several females of a pride have cubs the same age.

As soon as young male lions become sexually mature, they are chased away from the pride. They often join up with other males and roam around as nomads. If they are strong enough, they will challenge a dominant male to fight, with the aim of taking over a pride of their own. The mane of a young lion is a little sparse; the long, dark mane of a fully-grown lion signalizes strength and good health.

TOP ROW *Little baboons are a bit like human children. They run around screaming loudly, playing endless games and quarrelling with each other. Adolescents also take part in the chase.*
BOTTOM LEFT *Young baboons like to jump around on tree trunks, demonstrating their unbelievable climbing skills. As soon as they sense danger, the monkeys escape up trees. Here they also spend the night, protected from enemies.*
BOTTOM RIGHT *The newly born hang on tight to the fur of their mother. After about three weeks, they start to explore the world around them on their own. Mothers and aunts do not let them out of their sight, though, even whilst they groom each other.*

AGRICULTURE AT ITS LIMITS
A FARM IN NAMIBIA

WITH A LOOK OF INTENSE CONCENTRATION, Fred Jacobs watches a springbok through his binoculars. It is a fully-grown male. Fred reaches for his rifle, which has been specially made for him, aims and shoots. Even at a distance of 150 meters (490 feet), he hits his target – a perfect brain shot. The animal meets its death quickly and without much pain. It is bled and gutted there and then and the guts are left behind for the jackals. Then the dead animal is heaved into the truck. To show his respect for the life he has just taken, Fred spreads sand over the bloodstained ground. When back at the farm, he begins the procedure of skinning and cutting up the springbok in preparation for future mouth-watering meals. Hunting wildlife on ones own farmland is part of the way of life of Namibian farmers. Fred prefers to use the word "harvesting" rather than "hunting".

On our way back to the farmhouse, Fred shows us around his property. From the top of the red sand dunes, we get a good view over the wide grassy plains. It is a lovely piece of land. Repeatedly, we come across springboks, kudus, Oryx antelopes and steenboks. To us the size of the farm seems incredible. Back in Switzerland, an average farm only has 19 hectares (47 acres) of land. Fred has 10,000 hectares (24,700 acres)! Moreover, Fred's farm is only a little larger than the average farm in southern Kalahari.

Fred and his wife Onie have been passionate farmers for the past 30 years. They moved to southern Kalahari three years ago to develop Bagatelle Ranch as a sheep farm. You need a minimum average rainfall of 180 millimeters (7 inches) per year to run a farm with 1,500 sheep and remain in profit, but since the year 2000, the southern Kalahari has received much less rain than that. Therefore, two years ago, Fred and Onie decided to convert the farm into a wilderness farm, but not primarily for the production of meat. Today tourists from all over the world can stay in one of their ten lovingly furnished bungalows, which they built on the red dunes. Qualified guides introduce them to the secrets of the Kalahari. By combining their wilderness farm with tourism and keeping a few sheep to cover their own needs for meat, they can run it in an environmentally sustainable and profitable manner. Meanwhile the farm employs 24 people. Fred considers his responsibility for his employees as the biggest challenge in his new business.

In the very dry southern Kalahari, only sheep can be bred. The stock of Kohus van der Westhuizen is neutered, marked and vaccinated against ticks and other parasites.

In the area around Gobabis in Namibia, the average annual rainfall is around 450 millimeters (17.5 inches). This is sufficient for breeding cattle. Food and water, however, are only sufficient for extensive meat production; milk production is not possible. The animals are usually left to their own devices, roaming around the countryside. Typically, the farms are huge compared to European standards, and are run by only a few farmhands.

TOP LEFT *Othmar, a laborer of the cattle farmer Sieglinde Nauhaus, milks the cows in the morning. The milk is needed on the farm.*
BOTTOM LEFT *Sylvester and Abraham carve up a springbok at the Bagatelle Kalahari Game Ranch. The meat is turned into a delicious meal for the guests.*

TOP RIGHT *A half-tame group of meerkats inhabit Bagatelle Kalahari Game Ranch. The mother of the lively clan was bottle-fed by Onie Jacobs, the owner of Bagatelle.*
BOTTOM RIGHT *A laborer marks the sheep and goats, which were sold at an animal auction near Gobabis in Namibia.*

TOP ROW *The Bagatelle Kalahari Game Ranch has successfully switched from a sheep farm to a wilderness farm catering for tourists. Imelda prepares the guest rooms every day. The guests are invited for a drink in the former farmhouse. Fred Jacobs, the owner of Bagatelle, has shot a springbok on his farm.*
BOTTOM LEFT *On a cool winter night an endless canopy of stars spreads out above the bungalows of Bagatelle.*
BOTTOM RIGHT *Dwain, the manager of Bagatelle, expects his guests for dinner on the dune.*

Sebastian, a guide of the Bagatelle Kalahari Game Ranch, serves his "Sundowner" to the guests. He has just led them through the red dune landscape. Today many wild animals live on his farm, which has a size of 10,000 hectares (24,700 acres). Animal species, which were eradicated in this area during previous centuries, have been reintroduced again. On a small section of the farm, antelopes are still hunted for the farm's own needs.

The year 2006 brought more than the average amount of rain. Consequently, the red sandy ground is densely covered with grass. "With these rains we could have kept the farm," Fred says a little wistfully. However, climatologists have already predicted a new drought for Southern Africa in the coming year. It is linked to the El Niño phenomenon, a rise in temperatures of the Pacific. The droughts, which are getting longer and longer, represent an existential threat to many farmers in the Kalahari who already have a very hard time reaping any harvest from the barren land. Therefore, many Namibian farmers are forced to seek additional ways of earning their income.

Fred's 70-year old neighbor Pieter van der Westhuizen is an impressive example of someone equipped with an innovative spirit and a lot of dedication. Pieter is trying to

cultivate the plant *Hoodia gorgonii*. In times of drought, the Bushmen used to chew on this plant to suppress their feelings of hunger. P57, the active constituent of *Hoodia gorgonii*, is now used in diet pills in the western world. This is a million dollar business and the Bushmen have succeeded in claiming part of it in a lengthy legal battle over their intellectual property rights. If the plant could be cultivated successfully, the illegal collection of this rare plant would stop. Pieter plans to share his results with the Bushmen to help them get into the cultivation business themselves.

Further north, in the central Kalahari, the average rainfall is a little more – around 300 to 450 millimeters (12 to 17.5 inches). This is sufficient for cattle to find enough food. We pay a visit to the cattle farmer Sieglinde Nauhaus who lives near Gobabis. In common with

Sieglinde Nauhaus runs a cattle farm near Gobabis. She has German ancestors from the period when Namibia was still called Deutsch-Südwestafrika and was a colony of Germany. In common with 30,000 other Namibians of German descent, she speaks German and listens daily to the German radio program. But if she meets other farmers, she can switch between German, English and Afrikaans effortlessly.

many white cattle farmers in Namibia, the family Nauhaus has German ancestors. Sieglinde runs her farm of 7,000 hectares (17,290 acres) and 500 cattle with the help of only three employees. To operate the farm sustainably, she refrains from holding more stock than one animal per 15 hectares (37 acres). The cattle graze around so-called cattle posts, where water is pumped into troughs for them. When they have grazed the area around one cattle post, they are herded to the next. To this day horses are still used to herd, mark and vaccinate them. Likewise, these procedures occur on the farm of Sieglinde Nauhaus's daughter Karin, too, where we accompany the cowboys driving 30 cattle to their new owner. We feel as if we are in the Wild West. Sieglinde Nauhaus, on the other hand, transports her cattle from one post to the next by truck. This way she can trick her animals when it is time to be taken to the slaughterhouse. They are transported to the slaughterhouse in the same truck; but as they are used to this vehicle, they will not notice what is brewing, therefore, will not become agitated. The meat stays tender longer if the animals do not produce fear hormones prior to being slaughtered.

Meat, which is produced extensively and in a natural way in Namibia, tastes fantastic. It is exported to the EU as well. Nonetheless, agriculture makes up only five per cent of the gross national product, although over a third of the population earns their living in this sector. Mainly the 4,500 white farmers use a little less than half the agricultural land commercially. Only every tenth farm belongs to a non-white farmer. The other half of the agricultural land is occupied by 150,000 households which get by with subsistence agriculture, mainly animal husbandry. It is clear that there is the need for a more just distribution of land. The implementation of the Land Reform Act, introduced in 1995, is one of the important political challenges of Namibia.

Pieter van der Westhuizen tries to cultivate Hoodia gorgonii on his farm near Marienthal in the south of Namibia. Unfortunately, the ground squirrels ate most of the seedlings planted outside. This plant contains a natural agent, which helped the Bushmen suppress their hunger when times were tough. Today the pharmaceutical industry uses this agent in diet pills.

Before giraffes drink, they survey the surrounding area. They can spot a lion several kilometers (miles) away. Only once they are certain that there is no danger, they pluck up the courage to drink. Grown giraffes can defend themselves very effectively and are not attacked very often. They can give a predator a fatal kick with their hooves. Lions or hyenas however, sometimes kill young giraffes.

Giraffes belong to those animals who can best deal with drought. They survive for weeks without having to drink. They make do with the moisture in the leaves which they feed on. In addition, they conserve the water that their body contains. Their body temperature can increase by ten degrees without perspiring. Whilst breathing, they also minimize the loss of water. When they exhale, the moisture is condensed and thus retained on its way through the long neck.

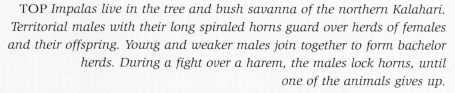

TOP *Impalas live in the tree and bush savanna of the northern Kalahari. Territorial males with their long spiraled horns guard over herds of females and their offspring. Young and weaker males join together to form bachelor herds. During a fight over a harem, the males lock horns, until one of the animals gives up.*

RIGHT *The female impalas watch their surroundings carefully. They are the prey of many carnivores. Leopards, lions, hyenas, African wild dogs, jackals and crocodiles, hunt them. Flight is their survival strategy. When they flee they keep on jumping high into the air – up to nine meters (approx. 30 feet) far and three meters (10 feet) high. Presumably, this is to help them orientate themselves and keep a constant check on the whereabouts of their pursuers.*

A LIFE FOR THE CHEETAHS
THE CHEETAH CONSERVATION FUND

CHEWBACCA'S MUSCLES TENSE, THEN HE IS OFF! In just a few seconds, he accelerates to almost 100 kilometers (60 miles) per hour. He provides an impressive demonstration that he is a member of the fastest mammal species in the world. This time however, he is not chasing an antelope! It is an old rag. This is part of the Cheetah Conservation Fund's (CCF) training program for this half-tamed cheetah. As an ambassador of his kind, Chewbacca helps to persuade people to get involved in the conservation of cheetahs. Since 1995, he has been supporting Laurie Marker, the foundress of the CCF, in this mission. Laurie adopted him as a three-week-old orphan and raised him herself. She named him after the Star Wars figure Chewbacca. His name stands for the battle to save the world.

With their slim bodies and long legs, cheetahs are built for speed. When they hunt, they quietly stalk their prey, approach it as closely as possible and then attack in full sprint. Equipped with tough pads on their paws and with claws that act like spikes they can accelerate like a Ferrari; but contrary to the racing car, which can only keep up high speeds on a straight track, cheetahs can change direction within mere fractions of a second when chasing antelopes. However, after a few hundred meters (less than a half mile) the cheetah must have brought its prey to fall, as then its strength starts to dwindle. Every second hunting attempt is rewarded by success. After hunting, a cheetah is often so exhausted that it has to rest for up to half an hour before hurriedly devouring his kill. The disadvantages of the very specialized lightweight build of the cheetah are weak jaws and small teeth. Consequently, cheetahs do not have a chance in defending their kill against larger predators such as lions, leopards and hyenas. This is why cheetahs have a hard time in conservation areas, where its larger competitors start to increase in numbers.

Around 95 percent of the cheetahs of Namibia share their habitat with commercial farmers and their livestock. Throughout the last century, they were hunted as vermin and killed by the thousands. In 1975, the cheetah was placed on the Red List of Endangered Species. Only since the mid 90's has its numbers started to stabilize. Although illegal killing has still not stopped completely, many farmers in Namibia have now changed their attitude towards this endangered species.

Cheetahs hunt during the day. From the vantage point of trees or termite hills, they keep a lookout for potential prey.

In 1990, the American Laurie Marker founded the conservation organization Cheetah Conservation Fund in central Namibia. Prior to that, she worked in a zoo in Oregon and was involved with breeding cheetahs and reintroducing them into the wild. She quickly found that the cats were hard to breed in captivity and those animals which she reintroduced into the wild in Namibia were shot by the farmers. So she started to focus on the remaining wild populations of cheetah and the question of how humans and wild animals can live peacefully in Namibia.

TOP LEFT *A small head, weak jaws and small teeth are the price a cheetah pays for a body which is built for speed. The cheetah can judge distances with accuracy thanks to the position of its eyes: high up and directed forwards.*

TOP RIGHT *Laurie Marker raised the cheetah Chewbacca herself, after a farmer shot his mother.*

BOTTOM LEFT *After training, Chewbacca is rewarded with a piece of meat.*

BOTTOM RIGHT *At the CCF cheetah orphans are kept in large outdoor pens. As they have never learnt to hunt themselves, they cannot be introduced into the wilderness anymore. To ensure that they stay fit, although they are fed, Bonnie und Mandy Schumann train them with a running maschine.*

TOP ROW *Cheetahs are the fastest mammals in the world. Their extremely flexible spine allows them to make bounds of ten meters (33 feet).*
BOTTOM LEFT *Their huge lungs and nostrils of more than average size ensures that their body is supplied with sufficient oxygen while sprinting.*
BOTTOM RIGHT *The enormous exertion of strength needed limits their endurance. Cheetahs can only sustain their top speed of over 100 kilometers (60 miles) per hour for a few hundred meters.*

95 percent of the cheetahs in Namibia live on farms beyond protected areas. They were hunted and killed for decades. Meanwhile it has been shown, that a cheetah will always prefer wild animals to domestic ones. Consequently, if there is enough wild prey on the farm, the losses of livestock decrease dramatically. And even if a cheetah does occasionally kill a calf, shooting a cheetah will not solve the problem, since, as soon as he is removed, several rivaling cheetahs will intrude into his territory which is now no longer occupied.

With 3,000 cheetahs, Namibia has the largest cheetah population in the world. This is thanks to a very dedicated woman with a vision.

When Laurie Marker came to Namibia for the first time in 1977, she was convinced that the re-introduction of cheetahs, formerly kept in zoos, back into the wilderness could support their survival. However, she quickly realized that she had been gravely wrong. The re-introduced animals immediately faced the same threat as their wild counterparts: the threat of being hunted and killed by farmers. In 1990 therefore, Laurie Marker founded the Cheetah Conservation Fund (CCF) in central Namibia. Within 15 years, she turned the CCF into a well-known center for the conservation of cheetahs, combining research and edu-

cation. She sought personal contact with the farmers to deal with the hunting problem. She saw that only the farmers themselves could save the cheetahs. "Namibia's farmers are very close to nature," Laurie told us. "Some of them are great conservationists." Laurie managed to prove to them that cheetahs primarily hunt wild prey. Therefore, enough wild prey on the farm to hunt would lead to a reduction in the loss of livestock. Even if a cheetah occasionally killed a calf, the solution to the problem though, would not be to shoot it, as then several rivaling cheetahs would enter his former territory.

Small livestock and young animals require particular protection. By supplying the farmers with sheep dogs, Laurie provides them with a concrete solution to this problem.

Aside from being hunted by humans, all the cheetahs today have descended from a small group of animals. The consequences of this incest are high cub mortality and a small number of sperm; moreover, approximately 70 per cent of the sperm cells are deformed. Genetic diversity, though, is the prerequisite for an animals' ability to adapt to new environmental conditions and to survive threats such as epidemics. Cheetahs, unfortunately, are ill equipped for either.

Since 1994, the CCF has been breeding and training Anatolian sheep dogs. We visit the little puppies, which grow up amongst a herd of goats. They playfully measure their strength with the young kids as though they were goats themselves. We have to resist the urge to stroke these cute little puppies, as they are not supposed to become too familiar with humans. They are meant to develop a strong bond with the herd so they can defend it later as adults, against predatory animals, such as the cheetah. The barking dogs drive away the shy cheetahs easily.

One of the handicaps of the cheetahs is that they only have a very limited genetic diversity. They were on the brink of extinction worldwide when the climate changed around 10,000 years ago. All of the cheetahs today derive from a very small group. Therefore, they are closely related to each other and genetically very similar. The consequences of this are malformations and slow-moving sperms. A deadly virus could wipe out all cheetahs in any one area. That is why cheetah sperm is frozen and preserved for future use at the CCF.

Aside from research, Laurie considers education as vital. "Children are our hope for the future," she says. This is why the CCF is actively involved in environmental education. Laurie Marker and Chewbacca have become world-famous through their work. Together they fight for the survival of the cheetahs and for a world where humans and animals share a living space. "Love for animals alone is not enough," Laurie explains. "It is more important to cooperate with those that are affected. People living in poverty do not see any sense in nature and animal conservation." Therefore, her greatest challenge is to understand the needs of the people. With innovative projects, she is finding ways of combining cheetah conservation with opening up new sources of income for the local population.

Cheetahs are a severely endangered species worldwide. Thanks to the protection of cheetahs, Namibia's population has increased to 3,000 animals again.

PAGE 88/89 Giraffes in the Central Kalahari Game Reserve.

"God is really only another artist.
He invented the giraffe, the elephant,
and the cat. He has no real style.
He just keeps on trying other things."

PABLO PICASSO,
SPANISH ARTIST
(1881-1973)

THE SALTPANS

THE HUGE SALTPAN SHIMMERS WHITE IN THE MIDDAY HEAT. The sun beats down mercilessly; there is no shade anywhere, which might provide some relief. On the horizon, endlessly far away, we can see the curvature of our planet. The glimmering plain merges with the blue sky. There is an almost eerie silence. All you can hear is the wind blowing hauntingly across this barren pan. After it cools down in the evening, the wind picks up and develops gale forces, howling unimpeded across this extra-terrestrial landscape. The saltpans, formed by the drying up of former water holes and lakes, are an absolute hostile environment in the dry season. Merely springboks and Oryx antelopes turn up here to lick salt.

However, when the rains finally come, the water replenishes the saltpans again. Millions of small organisms, which have survived the drought in eggs, hatch now. This plentiful food resource attracts hundreds of thousands of birds from all over Africa. Nutritious grasses grow around the saltpans. This is where huge herds of wildebeest and zebras gather, their predators following shortly thereafter. The wildebeest defy them by giving birth to their calves almost simultaneously. Ninety percent of all females calve within a period of three weeks. This is the beginning of a time of plenty for the lions, hyenas and jackals. Nevertheless, even during the short period when the newly born calves are defenseless, they can only kill a small proportion of the large numbers.

There are countless saltpans in the Kalahari. One of them is the Makgadikgadi Pan. With its 12,000 square kilometers (4,632 square miles) it is the largest in the world. In the past, when people did not yet have maps, they traveled from saltpan to saltpan. The pans not only served as landmarks, people could successfully dig for water along their edges. This is why the first settlements in southern Africa developed around saltpans.

The Makgadikgadi pans have a total area of 12 000 square kilometer (4,632 suare miles). This is
the largest area of saltpan in the world.

PAGE 92/93 *Herd of springboks in the Etosha National Park.*

Lions stalk their prey. In the vicinity of large herds of animals, you will often find a pride of them in hiding. Male lions weigh more than 200 kilos. They are too heavy to make good hunters, so it is mainly the more agile females who do the hunting. But with regard to feeding, the males enjoy the advantage of being the stronger sex.

Zebras live in harems led by a strong stallion. They spend the dry season near permanent water holes. In the wet season, they form large herds and set of to fresh pastures. The foals are courageously defended by the whole harem, but especially by the stallion. Lions therefore, more seldom kill young zebras.

AT THE LAKE OF TEARS
A WATERHOLE ON THE ETOSHA PAN

WE STARE INTO THE DARKNESS, FULL OF SUSPENSE. We can only just make out a silhouette. This time it is not an optical illusion playing games with our overstrained eyes. A grey hulk of a creature lumbers towards the water. While it drinks, the Black Rhino seems to be watching us with his small beady eyes; but probably it detected our scent, as its eyesight is poor. It can hardly see further than 20 meters (65 feet) ahead. When a second rhino approaches, the first one stamps the ground, whirling up a cloud of dust – no doubt in an effort to impress the potential opponent. The two competitors move towards each other in slow motion, staring into each other's eyes for minutes on end, trying to weigh up one another's strength. Suddenly one of them makes a bolt for it. It looks like rhinos subscribe to the philosophy of using insight prior to violence.

We enjoy the show at the floodlit water hole of Okaukuejo in Etosha National Park. Here tourists get the unique opportunity to watch the creatures of the night from a close but safe distance. The animals themselves neither seem to mind the light nor the people sitting on benches behind a low stone wall.

In the language of the Ovambo, Etosha means great, white place. According to a legend of the Haicom Bushmen, endless streams of tears that a young mother shed after strangers had murdered her child, created the lake. The dried up lake of tears, a saltpan of 5,000 square kilometers (1,930 square miles), represents the heart of the park. This salt desert gradually extends into grass, bush and tree savanna. There are numerous water holes around the southern edge of the pan, which contain water all year round. This is where many animals migrate in the dry season. Second to the Serengeti, the Etosha National Park in the north of Namibia is the region of Africa with the most wildlife. With a total area of 22,275 square kilometers (8,598 square miles), it is half the size of Switzerland!

Meanwhile a herd of elephants has gathered at our water hole. They immediately become the kings of the castle. A young bull squirts water over the rhino until it gets so fed up that finally it vacates. Dust clouds mingle with the smell of the sulphurous elephant farts.

In the evening, the tourists of Etosha National Park in Namibia gather at the floodlit water holes to watch the nocturnal animals.

Shortly after sunset, a herd of elephants visits the water hole at Okaukuejo. Temporarily these gray giants take over the scene. It is noisy and dusty. After half an hour, the spectacle is over. The leading cow leads her herd back into the black night. The tourists sitting behind the low stone wall wait for the next attraction.

TOP LEFT *An exciting nocturnal encounter: a family of elephants comes across a rhino mum and her calf on its way to the waterhole at Halali.*

TOP RIGHT *A bull shows interest in the rhino mother and her offspring. The two grown Black Rhinos stare into each other's eyes for minutes on end. The encounter remains peaceful. Presumably, the rhino bull is the father of the little one.*

BOTTOM LEFT *Black Rhinos only start to get active by night. This is when the loners wander to the water hole one after the other. There is no better place to watch these rare animals than the floodlit water holes in Etosha National Park.*

BOTTOM RIGHT *A young elephant bull makes a threatening charge at two Black Rhinos. He cannot tolerate any rivalry at the water hole.*

One by one, Egyptian Slit-faced Bats fly out of a rock crevice on the hill at Halali. The bats have spent the day in their dark cave. They do not feel comfortable in the dry, hot climate. Only when night falls do they come out to hunt for insects, equipped with their own sonar system. Later they will fly to their roost for the night where they groom themselves and catch spiders and scorpions.

On March 22, 2007, the Etosha National Park, one of the oldest national parks in Africa, celebrated its centennial. When founded, it was four times the size it is today; but during this period, there was hardly any wildlife. Poaching and big game hunting in the 19th century nearly eradicated all animals. As the animal population recovered in the course of the following centuries, the requirements for land of the local people and the white settlers grew. As a result, the size of the park was reduced several times, without any regard for the animals. In 1973, the park was fenced in. The Kaokoveld, the most important region for the rare Black Rhino, was suddenly outside of the park. To save the rhinos from poachers, 52 of them were caught and released again within the park boundaries.

Meanwhile, back at our water hole, the elephants have disappeared into the night again. A couple of jackals prance around. A giraffe approaches cautiously. In the distance, we can hear hyenas howling. Later they come to drink, too. Most of the tourists have disappeared into their bungalows or tents by this time. After midnight, there is not much going on at the waterhole. Occasionally a Black Rhino turns up to drink. It is freezing cold. At the crack of dawn, around 5.30 am, we are still sitting on the green wooden bench, cold stiff.

Things start to liven up again at the waterhole with the first rays of warm morning sun. Guinea fowl, springboks, wildebeest and oryx antelopes arrive to quench their thirst. In daylight, the animals that fear the lions during darkness daringly emerge. Towards noon,

Ten glowing eyes stare at the rhino mother and her offspring. Five male lions lie in hiding in the scrub. But Black Rhinos are no easy prey, particularly the grown ones; they can defend themselves viciously. The lions therefore focus on their calves. If they succeed in isolating one of them from their mother, it would mean certain death. – However, the lions take a high risk in attacking rhinos.

the zebras arrive in a seemingly endless procession. After 24 hours of suspense at the waterhole, we managed to see all the animals, except for the predators of the night.

On the drive to Halali Camp the next morning, we do not see a single Black Rhino. These night-active loners have retreated under a shady bush for the day. However, as if to compensate us for that, three lionesses lie in front of us on the warmed up road. Their bloody mouths bear witness to a successful night. Close by there are grazing zebras. Thousands of them populate the lush grassy plains following the big rains. On the horizon, giraffes move from one acacia tree to the next.

In Halali we spend the evening at the flood-lit water hole, too. We wait for more than an hour, but nothing happens. Some of the more impatient tourists get bored and leave. Then suddenly five young male lions arrive silently. They lie in wait, forming a semi circle. Our tension rises when a mother rhino appears with her young one. There is no way we want to miss this, so we skip dinner. The lions start to circle the rhinos. The defensive mother confronts them courageously, determined by whatever means to protect her offspring. She instinctively knows that the worst thing she could possibly do would be to run away. It is a stalemate situation: lions and rhinos face each other without moving. A mere lapse of concentration would be certain death for her little one. After more than an hour, the lions finally give up. The risk of attacking is too high. They disappear into the night to look for easier prey.

By night, the giraffes are particularly careful at the water holes. They are somewhat vulnerable when they drink; with their legs spread wide they can easily be attacked by lions. Two giraffes therefore check out the surroundings whilst the third one drinks.

TOP *Two elephant bulls in Etosha National Park are powdered white after their mud and dust bath.*
RIGHT *Following the extensive dust bath of an elephant family, a fine white cloud hovers over the plains for a long time.*

PAGE 106/107 *Some of the enormous baobabs on Lekhubu Island, in the middle of the Makgadikgadi Salt Pan, are probably more than one thousand years old. The Scottish explorer of Africa, David Livingstone, described these strange trees as huge, upturned carrots.*

WITNESSES OF TIME
MYTHICAL BAOBAB TREES

AFTER GOD HAD CREATED ALL THE ANIMALS, he gave each one of them a sapling to plant so that Earth would become lush and green. When it was the hyena's turn, God presented it with its plant accompanied by the stern words: "You have to control your malice and quit stealing." The hyena stubbornly refused. Thus, God made it stand at the end of the queue and finally, when it was its turn again, gave it a left over baobab tree. The hyena was furious, so planted the tree upside down. According to this myth of the Bushmen, the baobab has been growing the wrong way around ever since, stretching its roots towards the sky.

We feel small and insignificant sitting beneath the largest tree in Botswana, Chapman's Baobab. We try to picture how a family of Bushmen would have set up camp in its shade 2500 years ago. In the 18th century, the tree served as a landmark in the monotonous landscape of the Makgadikgadi saltpan. You can spot it from a distance of 20 kilometers (12 miles). Explorers and traders of Africa also used this tree as a post office. They left their messages in cavities in its trunk. Many carved their names into its smooth bark. The initials JC are those of the British explorer James Chapman, who traveled through this part of Africa in the second half of the 19th century. The massive trunk of the baobab has a circumference of 25 meters (82 feet). It can store up to 9000 liters (approx. 2800 gallons) of water. This is how Chapman's Baobab can survive long periods of drought and devastating bushfires.

Elephants love baobabs. They use their tusks to rip open the bark to try to get at the moist fibers in the trunk. The trees seem to survive this torture. The Bushmen, too, used to tap the water reserves of the baobabs. To this day, the people of the Kalahari utilize almost every part of the tree. They dry its fruit, which is rich in vitamins and calcium and make it into a powder. This powder can be stored for long periods of time and added to water to help people get through the dry season without suffering from vitamin deficiency. They suck the seeds like sweets or grind them into a kind of coffee powder. The young leaves are cooked like vegetables and have a similarity to spinach. The bark is also used to make string, ropes, nets, mats, baskets, hats, clothes and paper. The only thing they cannot use the baobab for is firewood. It simply contains too much water.

In 1862, the English explorer and painter Thomas Baines painted the Baines Baobabs in the Nxai Pan Nationalpark. Since that time they have not changed much, they have only lost one branch!

In the south of the Sahara, African baobabs grow in dry savannah. Outside of Africa, in northwestern Australia only one species of baobab can be found, and six further species can be found on Madagascar. Baobabs do not make too many demands on the ground they grow on. On Lekhubu Island, they seem to grow straight from the rock. The baobab's dense network of roots does not go deep, but it spreads over a large area. It helps the tree to optimize the amount of water it can absorb following one of the rare rainfalls.

There is a group of baobabs in the Nxai Pan National Park called the Seven Sisters. The British painter Thomas Baines painted them in 1862. They have not changed at all; they look just the same today as they do in his painting – standing at the edge of the Kudiakam saltpan where they defy transience. Baines' could easily have painted his picture yesterday.

Before the rains come, the baobab develops leaves in its finely branched crown. Only a few weeks later large white blossoms with a disagreeable scent will develop, opening up at dusk. Flying foxes, a large species of bat, are strongly attracted to the smell. They pollinate the tree by flying from blossom to blossom to lick the nectar. The very same night, after pollination, the blossoms drop to the ground. Large oval fruits develop, these being

a favorite food for baboons, antelopes and elephants. Without realizing it, these animals spread the seed of the baobab.

On the small granite island of Lhekubu, in the middle of the endless expanse of the Makgadikgadi Pan, ancient, strange baobabs seem to be growing straight from the rocks. Elephants must have spread the seeds of the trees to this place several thousands of years ago. We decide to set off for that island. Near Gweta we reach the former shoreline of what used to be Africa's largest lake; its former size being approximately 60,000 square kilometers (23,000 square miles). This is 100 times the size of Lake Constance, bordered by Switzerland, Austria and Germany. 10,000 years ago, Lake Makgadikgadi finally dried out

If you pick the flower of a baobab, be prepared to be eaten by a lion! On the other hand, water in which the seeds of the baobab have been soaked is supposed to protect you from crocodile attacks. No other tree in Africa is at the center of so many myths and legends.
Apart from that, baobabs represent a place to meet in African villages; much like the role that linden and oak trees played in medieval villages in central Europe. Markets and meetings are still held under baobabs and feasts are celebrated under them, too.

completely, leaving behind the saltpan as we know it today. Only in the wet season does it hold water. But towards the end of the winter, the pan is so dry that we can drive across it without any risk of sinking into moist and soft salt mud. After driving across white expanses and grassy islands devoid of any human habitation for hours on end, Lhekubu Island finally appears on the horizon. We feel as though we have finally arrived at the end of the world. We immediately climb the highest point of the island to get a view, which is only 50 meters (164 feet) above the salt sea: absolute emptiness surrounds us. Just like the lake it was before; the white salt plain dissolves in its vastness. Along its former shores we find pebbles, which have been worn smooth by the waves. The cliffs on the island are covered in white bird droppings. We only find out later that these are the fossil remains of a bird colony which fed on the fish from the lake 10,000 years ago. In the light of the setting sun, the trees turn purple, then grey. The temperatures drop dramatically. But close to a baobab, it remains comfortably warm. The tree seems to radiate the heat that it has absorbed during the day.

Up until 1950, Bushmen populated the island. They worshipped Lekhubu Island as a holy place where God was said to have lived beneath the cliffs. Even today, they come to this place to make offerings and pray to him for rain. Clay shards and tools from the Stone Age, more than 20,000 years old, provide evidence that the place was also inhabited at a much earlier time. There are remains of a round wall of stone, presenting a mystery unsolved. It is estimated to be more than 1,000 years old. It is thought that maybe initiation rites of the Bantu tribes were performed here. The baobabs could probably tell us the true story!

Many adventurers and explorers, over the last few centuries, have set up camp for the night under the Baines Baobabs. Looking south from here the nocturnal star-spangled sky seems to rotate around an imaginary Southern Star.

TOP *The springboks in Nxai Pan National Park form large herds of several hundred animals during the wet season.*
RIGHT *Wildebeest migrate to the edge of the Sowa Pan to lick salt. In the rainy season, they encounter tens of thousands of flamingos at the shallow salt lake.*

PAGE 115/116 *After good years of rain, thousands of zebras populate the grassy plains of Etosha National Park.*

TOP ROW *Banded mongooses hunt for insects and millipedes during the day. Families of up to 30 animals sometimes wander through the Camps of Etosha National Park. Black-backed jackals live and hunt in couples. They also raise their pups together. Young Bat-eared Foxes wait at the burrow, while their parents with the large ears forage for beetles and insect larvae.*

BOTTOM LEFT *In the early morning a leopard takes a short break in the branches of a fallen over tree near Namutoni in Etosha National Park, before it retreats to its hide-out for the day.*

BOTTOM RIGHT *Female lions occupy the same territory for generations. Males are usually chased away again by stronger competitors after only two years.*

A PINK SEA
FLAMINGOS

THE SKY COLORS THE ENDLESS SALT LAKE A DEEP BLUE. The towers of clouds reflected on its mirror-like surface. Romantic bays with white beaches are reminiscent of the South Sea. The birds dance their longest legs in the world, in its depths of only a few centimeters. 200,000 delicate pink flamingos sweep their curved bills through the mud, filtering out algae and crustaceans, quacking contentedly.

We are both surprised and relieved to find that the Sowa Salt Pan, one of the Makgadikgadi pans, is full of water; but it has not seen one drop of rain in this rainy season. The water in the pan is from last year's rains when Botswana experienced record downpours. This year the flamingos did not leave, due to there being enough water available for them to stay right through the dry season. Rain transforms the barren saltpan into a shallow, nutrient-rich lake. Within no time at all the water teems with millions of microscopic algae and bacteria. Crustaceans hatch from their resistant permanent eggs. Usually tens of thousands of flamingos arrive almost simultaneously with the rains. It is a mystery how they know when the rains will come to Botswana, when they are hundreds of kilometers (miles) away.

Two of the five species of flamingos worldwide can be found in Africa. These two species share the same habitat, but do not share the same diet. The Lesser Flamingo mainly strains blue-green algae from the water. These blue-green algae contain carotenes, which give the flamingos their pink color. Greater Flamingos on the other hand primarily strain small crustaceans from the salt mud. They consume the pink pigment indirectly by feeding mainly on the crustaceans, which in turn feed on the blue-green algae. Both species of flamingo use their bills like ladles. With their tongues, they pump water in and out of it. The bills are equipped with hairy lamellae and, depending on their size and alignment, algae or crustaceans are caught on them. The birds spend up to 15 hours a day with their heads down and their bills in the water.

In the evening the flamingos, which have spent the day wading around calmly, become more active. They move towards each other purposefully. Lesser and Greater Flamingos gather in several groups. The peaceful quacking develops a more excited tone,

See page 124

Rain turns the normally so barren salt desert of the Sowa Pan into a shallow lake full of nutrients.
Lesser Flamingos spend 15 hours a day filtering algae from the water – head first.

TOP ROW *At sunset, the pink wings of flying flamingos glow in the last rays of light. In the evening they migrate back to their breeding colony, 50 kilometers (30 miles) away, to feed their chicks. Lesser Flamingos (center) and Greater Flamingos (right) assemble in separate groups before they set off.*

BOTTOM LEFT *The half-grown white flamingos hatched a year ago. Only when they are fully-grown do they turn pink through the carotenoids, which they take up with their food.*

BOTTOM RIGHT *At night, the flamingos wade or fly out into the lake, away from the shore. Here there is less chance of encountering predators.*

The Tswana of Botswana call flamingos "thunder and lightning". Almost simultaneously with the first proper summer thunderstorms they fly in from all over southern Africa. Up to ten thousand of them will then populate the water-filled saltpans. The shallow salt lake of the Sowa Pan contains more nutrients than any other lake in Africa. The rapidly reproducing algae and small planktonic fauna make it a "Land of Plenty" for the flamingos.

becoming louder and louder, eventually transforming into strange metallic sounding cries. A first group takes to the air. In formation they fly south over our heads. Their pink wings shine in the last light of the setting sun. The other groups follow. Then calm returns to the bay again. "They fly to their breeding colony which is 50 kilometers (30 miles) away," the flamingo researcher Graham Mc Culloch tells us the next day. 90,000 chicks have hatched on an island in the middle of the southern Sowa Pan.

Flamingos often have life-long mates. They build cone-shaped mud hills, up to 40 centimeters high (16 inches), onto which the female lays one single egg. On this tower-like nest, the egg is protected from floods after heavy rainfalls. On top of that, the temperatures up here rarely exceed 35 degrees Celsius, even when they may be as high as 50 degrees Celsius closer to the ground. Just a few days after they have hatched, the chicks leave their

nest. Several adults take turns in looking after the offspring. The parents start to focus on foraging for food again. For the first two months, they feed their own chick, which they recognize by the sound it makes, with crop milk. This liquid is enriched with carotene and blood and is just as nutritious as the milk of mammals.

A 6 to 10 kilometer (3.5 to 6 miles) wide belt of water and mud surrounds the breeding colony at the southern end of the Sowa Pan and protects the young birds from predators. But as it has not rained yet this year, this protective belt rapidly dries out. In 2001, in similar conditions, the chicks set off on foot to try to reach the water in the north of the Sowa Pan, 50 kilometers (30 miles) away. Only 3,000 of them survived this strenuous migration; but such a mass migration of flamingo chicks is a rare event. Graham Mc Culloch only experienced this twice in the course of the past eight years. Sometimes the chicks

On average, the flamingos only encounter suitable breeding conditions in the Sowa Pans every three years. Not every attempt at breeding is successful. Often the parents desert their chicks as the saltpan dries out too quickly. But such years of loss are compensated for by successful breeding years. Climate change with more frequent dry years, however, could seriously threaten the future of the flamingos in southern Africa.

wander off in all directions without any coordination and quickly fall prey to jackals and vultures. Only when adults lead them, do the chicks have any chance of reaching the life-saving water after a two-day march.

Graham does not expect these chicks to embark on such a migration. The rains are due any day now. This year Graham plans to ring flamingos in for the first time. He wants to ring 2,000 chicks to enable him to find out even more about them. At the end of March, just before the chicks leave their nests, he will be using lightweight quad bikes to get out to the breeding island. Dozens of helpers from southern Africa and Europe are on stand-by to assist him. When we meet Graham at the end of March however, all the flamingo chicks have died. The rains did not come after all. The water belt and the breeding colony dried up so quickly that jackals and hyenas managed to reach it as early as the end of February. The flamingo parents deserted their chicks. Maybe conditions were just too extreme for the chicks to attempt an exodus.

Flamingos are one of the oldest bird species. They have hardly changed in 30 million years. They are perfectly adapted to their habitat with its extreme fluctuations. Successful breeding years and complete losses are in balance with each other. Still, the drama in the Makgadikgadi Salt Pan weighs on us. As our climate changes, droughts will increase and the flamingos have nowhere to escape. There are only two other breeding places in Africa – Lake Natron in East Africa and the less suitable Etosha Pan in Namibia. Thus, a succession of years of drought could become an existential threat to the flamingos of southern Africa.

The salt lake of the Sowa Pan is only a few centimeters deep.
Because evaporation rates are high in the tropics, it usually
dries up again quickly after the wet season. Then it is time
for the flamingos to move on again.

PAGE 128/129 *According to the flamingo expert Graham*
Mc Culloch 200,000 flamingos were counted in the Sowa
Pan in the summer of 2006/7. This represents the entire
population of southern Africa. This large number is due to
good rains and a successful breeding season in the summer
of 2005/6.

"The so-called Desert, it may be observed, is by no means a useless tract of country. Besides supporting multitudes of both small and large animals, it sends something to the market of the world, and has proved a refuge to many a fugitive tribe ...."

DAVID LIVINGSTONE
BRITISH MISSIONARY AND EXPLORER
(1813-1873)
IN:
JOURNEYS AND RESEARCHES
IN SOUTH AFRICA

RIVERS

FINALLY, THE WATER STARTS TO FLOW AGAIN. Gradually the water level in the channels, enclosed by reeds and papyrus, rises. Sand banks and parched islands are submerged by the flood. Having traveled 1,800 kilometers (1,100 miles), the water from the highlands of Angola, where it rained heavily six months previously, has finally arrived. While the entire Kalahari suffers from drought, the swampy areas of the Okavango Delta double in size. The nutrients, which come down with the water, cause the largest inland delta on Earth to flourish. Whilst the tiger fish, a relation of the piranhas, migrate upstream to spawn at a secret place, the freshly hatched crocodiles populate the Delta downstream. Marabous, open-bill storks, storks and herons fly to their breeding islands in their thousands to commence their courtship.

Apart from the Okavango, there are only three other rivers in the Kalahari, which carry water throughout the year: the Chobe in the north of Botswana, the Zambezi that flows through Zambia and Zimbabwe and the Oranje River on the edge of the Kalahari in South Africa. During the dry season, these rivers represent arteries of life for animals and humans alike. Huge herds of animals gather along the Chobe, including herds of over 1,000 buffalo. Wherever buffalo graze, the lions are never far away. Every morning they deliver a merciless fight over life and death.

Two rivers have carved impressive landscapes into the otherwise flat Kalahari. In the North of South Africa, the Oranje thunders down a drop of 60 meters (197 feet) at the Augrabies Falls before it flows through a granite canyon 240 meters (787 feet) deep and 18 kilometers (11 miles) long. The Victoria Falls between Zambia und Zimbabwe is even mightier. This largest waterfall in Africa has eaten its way right into the black basalt.

Violent storms come down over the Okavango Delta at the beginning of the rainy season.

Chasing each other, diving and splashing with their mouths wide-open young hippos playfully learn to fight in a pool at the Khwai River. Although they are semi-grown already, their mother still takes care of them. Young hippos stay close to their mothers right up to sexual maturity at around six years of age.

Hippo bulls aggressively defend their territory against rivals. Whether to ward of enemies or when fighting or simply yawning, they can open their huge jaws up to an angle of 150 degrees. Their dangerously long canines continue to re-grow throughout their lives and are ground razor sharp by the teeth opposite. The lions at the Khwai River usually try to avoid grown hippos.

In a bird colony in the Okavango Delta male herons wait in the crowns of fig trees for females willing to mate. If a rival lands on the tree, it triggers loud quarrels. The numbers of herons are on the increase in Europe, too, although they were hunted mercilessly for a long time as they were seen to deplete fish stocks. Aside from fish, herons also like to feed on mice. They can often be seen in the meadows, motionlessly waiting for prey.

TOP LEFT *A Great Egret brings nest-making material to his nest.*
TOP RIGHT *The chicks of African Yellow-billed Storks need to be fed constantly. Both parents do nothing else for three weeks but feed their offspring, which rapidly increase in size.*

BOTTOM LEFT *During the breeding season, the Pink-backed Pelicans grow a tuft of feathers and their beaks, which are usually pink, turn a shade of yellow.*
BOTTOM RIGHT *Marabous start to nest at the end of the dry season, when many animals perish. During this time these carrion feeders find ample food. With a wingspan of nearly three meters (10 feet), they are almost as large as condors.*

THE SMOKE THAT THUNDERS
THE VICTORIA FALLS

DAVID LIVINGSTONE, THE FAMOUS SCOTTISH MISSIONARY and explorer of Africa, crawled right onto the very ledge of the waterfalls, when he "discovered" the Victoria Falls in 1855 as the first white man. In his diary he enthusiastically refers to the Falls as "... the most wonderful sight I had witnessed in Africa." Although, unlike many of his British explorer colleagues, he did not give every islet and every headland an English name, he made an exception in this case. In honor to his Queen, he named this majestic place "Victoria Falls".

The local Kololo people refer to the Victoria Falls as Mosi oa tunya – the smoke that thunders. You can see the cloud of spray, which can rise up to 400 meters (1,300 feet) high, from as far as 30 kilometers (18.6 miles) away. Livingstone wrote, "... we came in sight, for the first time, of the columns of vapor appropriately called 'smoke,' rising at a distance of five or six miles, exactly as when large tracts of grass are burned in Africa. Five columns now arose, and, bending in the direction of the wind, they seemed placed against a low ridge covered with trees; the tops of the columns at this distance appeared to mingle with the clouds." He immediately knew how this natural wonder had been formed. "The entire falls are simply a crack made in a hard basaltic rock from the right to the left bank of the Zambesi, and then prolonged from the left bank away through thirty or forty miles of hills."

With a length of 2,736 Kilometers (1,696 miles), the Zambezi is the longest river in Southern Africa. Its source lies in Zambia, on the borders to the Democratic Republic of the Congo and Angola. It flows through Zambia, Angola and Mozambique where it finally pours into the Indian Ocean. Upstream of the Victoria Falls, the Zambezi calmly meanders along with a width of up to two kilometers from bank to bank. Then its entire width suddenly crashes into a basalt canyon, 108 meters (354 feet) deep. When the Zambezi is in flood in April, around ten million liters of water cascade down per second. This largest waterfall in Africa is twice as high and one and half times as wide as the Niagara Falls.

Instead of approaching the Falls by canoe, as Livingstone did, we decide to hike it, along the trails of the small Victoria Falls National Park in Zimbabwe. We are amazed to find that we are suddenly surrounded by tropical rainforest. The lush green of the palm trees, ferns and strangler figs in the spray mist of the waterfalls seems like paradise. Long

In the spray of the Victoria Falls, a small tropical rainforest has developed in the otherwise dry Kalahari.

Mosi oa Tunya National Park protects the part of Victoria Falls, which lies in Zambia. It was here that the Scottish explorer Livingstone approached the edge of the Victoria Falls. When water flows are low, you can visit the precise spot on Livingston Island. Looking over from Zambia you get a view of the canyon wall opposite the Falls.

before we even catch a glimpse of the waterfalls, we can hear the roar of the water. When finally the forest gives way to a view of the Falls, we are simply overwhelmed by this natural spectacle, just as Livingstone was 150 years ago. Standing at the bottom of the canyon, we get a full view of the enormous water masses rushing down the opposite rock face. The water drops of spray glisten gold in the morning light. When the sun rises higher, a beautiful double rainbow appears, connecting both sides of the canyon.

"Scenes so lovely must have been gazed upon by angels in their flight," Livingstone wrote in his diary. Today flight operators use his words in their advertising campaigns. Flying over the Falls in a microlight we are simply awe struck. The almost two kilometer (1.24 miles) wide, calmly flowing Zambezi seems to abruptly disappear into a huge, smok-

ing crack of the Earth's crust, only to emerge again as a torrential stream roaring through the only narrow outlet – Batoka Gorge.

Over millions of years, the Zambezi dug its way through the thick basalt. Movements of the Earth's crust lead to several changes in its direction of flow. In places where cracks in the basalt were filled with softer sandstone, the river carved out eight waterfalls in the course of time. The canyons below today's Victoria Falls, which are arranged in a zigzag fashion, illustrate the way the Falls originally formed. A new cut in the rock indicates where the ninth waterfall will be several thousands of years from now.

In 1989, UNESCO declared the Victoria Falls a natural world heritage. Hardly anyone travels to Southern Africa without paying a visit to the Falls. Aside from wanting to

In the Victoria Falls National Park in Zimbabwe, a small trail leads around the canyon. Opposite, the water comes crashing down. You must be immune to vertigo to be able to look 100 meters (328 feet) into the depths from Danger Point. At so-called Boiling Pot, the water of Victoria Falls flows together before it is discharged through Batoka Canyon.

experience the unique natural landscape, nowadays, more and more tourists are keen on getting the adrenaline kick, which the Falls offer. The small town of Victoria Falls, which has very successfully been catering for adventure tourism during the last few years, is referred to as "Adrenaline City". Thirty percent of all tourists who come here spend a lot of money to buy their adventure. Some jump off the iron bridge above the Zambezi, secured by a long rubber band. This bridge is 111 meters (364 feet) high and connects Zimbabwe with Zambia. These people can pride themselves with having done the highest bungee jump in the world. Rafting is even more popular. Most visitors want to brave the notorious rapids of the Zambezi – just once in their lives. Every day hundreds of tourists equipped with a wetsuit, life vest and a helmet, are led down the steep iron staircase to the rubber rafts. When the water level is low, the adventure starts just downstream of Boiling Point where the river turns and heads down Batoka Gorge. Excited, nervous, but optimistic – this is what the passengers who set off one after another in the rafts, look like. But even after the first couple of rapids you can see them clinging on tightly to the ropes, soaked to the bone, screeching and squealing. I wonder what Livingstone, one of the pioneer adventurers, would have said to that.

When the water level is low in years of drought, the waterfall does not extend over its entire width of almost two kilometers (1.24 miles). Aside from this powerful and main waterfall however, only a few individual streams trickle down the basalt wall to the east.

PAGE 142/143 The rising sun paints the mist of the Victoria Falls' spray a tone of pastel pink. The spray can be seen from a long distance away.

Towards the end of the dry season, the flood from Angola finally
reaches the Khwai River in the southeastern part of the Okavango
Delta. Many of the large African animals migrate to the water then.
As opposed to the inner delta, this region of the Moremi Game Reserve
can also be accessed by car. Along the edge of the Okavango Delta,
mopane forests border onto seasonally flooded plains and lagoons.

From September on, the humidity starts to rise; then the intensity of the sun increases markedly on the southern edge of the tropical belt and from October on, the heat becomes almost unbearable. After months of deep blue, cloudless skies, more and more spectacular cloud formations start to develop. In a few weeks, they disperse as the first rains.

TOP *With their eyes, ears and nostrils set on top of their heads hippos can breathe even when almost entirely submerged and can survey the area discretely from this position. When they submerge completely they close both their nostrils and their ears.*

RIGHT *During the day, hippos spend most of their time in the water. Only when it cools down at night do they move onto land to graze.*

PAGE 148/149 *The tree skeletons on Dead Tree Island in Moremi Game Reserve bear testimony to the fact that this island must have been flooded in the past.*

COMBINED FORCES
THE BUFFALOES ON THE CHOBE RIVER

A MASSIVE BUFFALO, OBVIOUSLY WEIGHING SEVERAL TONS, blocks our path and fixates us with blood-shot eyes. Nostrils flared, it senses danger. Impressive horns point threateningly in our direction. Behind this colossus, we can see hundreds of buffalo migrating back into the bush, moving from the large floodplains of the Chobe in the early morning light. At the center of the herd, the females reside with the calves, protected by the massive bulls at the flanks. Soon we realize the buffalo is not fixating us. Glancing in our rear vision mirror, we spot a pride of lions, approaching slowly. Five lionesses are doing the same as we are: watching the herd of buffalo moving into the bush. They wait until there is just one straggler left, hobbling behind the herd. Then they attack! We cannot see a thing, as the fight is hidden in a cloud of dust. We had already given up hope for the poor buffalo when suddenly a group of them storm out of the bush. They initiate a furious counter-attack against the lionesses that flee in the face of their combined force.

The buffalo is one of the so-called Big Five, which also includes the elephant, the rhino, the lion and the leopard. Of all African animals, these are the most difficult to hunt, as they are the most dangerous to humans. Trophy hunters have pursued them mercilessly and have almost led them to extinction in several countries. On the other hand, more big game hunters have lost their lives to buffalo than to any other African animal. Nevertheless, stories about the buffalo's aggression are grossly exaggerated. Hunting accidents have usually involved injured animals. Buffaloes will only attack when cornered and see no means to escape.

During the dry season, several herds of up to 1,000 buffalo gather along the Chobe in the North of Botswana. At dawn, they move back into the bush from the floodplains, where they have spent the night grazing on the fresh grass. They spend the hot day in the shade, chewing the cud. Towards evening the herds make their way back to the river again.

Buffalo herds consist of families of several females and their offspring. A family is closely bonded; it protects the weakened, blind or injured members as well. Within the herd, young bulls stay together in bachelor groups. Older bulls remain alone or form small

See page 154

During the dry season, thousands of buffalo gather at the Chobe River in the north of Botswana.

Resting buffalo move close together in the high grass. As a compact herd, they are almost impossible to attack by lions. Only when they rise again to start grazing are they in danger, as now the lions can distinguish a weak or limping animal from a strong one.

TOP LEFT *The horns of the buffalo grow together to form a frontal shield.*
TOP RIGHT *Buffalo confirm their hierarchy by fighting against each other. But only when they fight over a female do they collide with each other with all their might. This force is comparable to that of a car crashing into a wall at a speed of 50 kilometers (31 miles) per hour!*

BOTTOM LEFT *Female buffalo also have horns, but lack the horn shield. They do not even try to challenge the bulls, as they are always the physically weaker. There is a separate hierarchy amongst the females.*
BOTTOM RIGHT *Buffalo calves start following their mothers very soon after having been born. Their mothers risk life and death to defend them against predators.*

In the evening, the buffalo herds migrate to the Chobe River. They spend the night grazing on the flood plains. The bull with the highest rank is guaranteed the best spot to graze at the front of the herd. The animals at the tail end of the herd have to make do with what the buffalo in front have left over. To make matters worse they are the prime target for lions.

groups a little distance away from the main herd. In both sexes, the dominance hierarchy is maintained by behavior such as head nodding, snorting and pawing the ground. The rank of an animal is determined by its size, strength and age. Females rise within the hierarchy if they have a calf in tow. Bulls always dominate the females due to their size alone. During the mating season, the bulls engage in violent fights over the females. They charge at each other, locking horns. Usually the fights are short and very quickly, there is a clear winner. Serious injuries are rare. A high rank gives an animal the right to graze at the head of the herd, within its center. Here the grass is less grazed and additionally the animals enjoy the highest protection from their enemies. The herd can be led by both sexes. High-ranking animals of both sexes take turns in taking command.

Buffalo are closely related to our cattle. Contagious diseases can be passed from one to the other. At the end of the 19th century, the rinderpest, which was brought in from Asia, wiped out almost all the cattle and buffalo in Africa. The result was a devastating famine, which affected large parts of the continent. Another one is the foot and mouth disease; harmless for African cattle and buffalo, but one of the most dreaded animal plagues in Europe. This is why the EU has very strict guidelines for the import of meat. The cattle of the export-orientated meat industry have to be separated from the wild buffalo, which carry the virus. In the middle of the 20th century, therefore, Botswana set up thousands of kilometers (miles) of cattle fences. A further disease, the bovine tuberculosis, is transmitted by a bacterium. In 1995, this disease spread from Namibia to Botswana. 320,000 cattle had to be

At dawn, the buffalo herds migrate from the floodplains of the Chobe back into the bush. There they spend the hottest time of the day in the shade ruminating.

slaughtered. The disease does not harm the cattle itself, but threatens the wild animal populations. Infected buffalo die and with them the predators, such as lions and hyena, who feed on their carcasses. To protect its animals from this disease Botswana set up cattle fences along its border to Namibia in the years following the plague.

These fences, however, intersected the habitats of wildlife and blocked their natural migratory routes. In the following droughts after 1980, hundreds of thousands of wildebeest and antelopes perished because of separation from water and their pastures. Botswana has learnt from this and has now changed its strategy. When setting up new cattle fences, natural animal migration routes are taken into consideration. A 40-kilometer (25 miles) wide wilderness corridor was reopened along the border between Botswana and Namibia.

Meanwhile dusk has fallen over the Chobe. Elephants and giraffes move leisurely across the wide plain. The first bull steps out of the bush carefully. Others follow. Soon several hundred animals surround us. In between the buffalo, white cattle egrets feed on the insects which have been stirred up by the herd. A group of oxpeckers descends on the buffalo to pick for parasites. It takes more than half an hour for the herd to move by on their way back to the fertile floodplains. A little nervously, we remember stories we have heard where buffalo have apparently trampled humans. But, we are relieved to experience buffalo as extremely peaceful and careful animals.

A buffalo cow moves in front of the herd – curiously, but carefully. If she comes across something she does not know, something a little disconcerting, she will prefer to make a detour around it.

PAGE 158/159 *In the morning and the evening the buffalo make good use of the crossing at the Chobe; it as an opportunity to drink.*

TOP *Nowadays the way to spend the nights in the bush is in a tent mounted on the car roof. These tents are easy to open and just as easy to pack up again.*

LEFT *In the south-west, the Kalahari borders on the Oranje River. In the South African Augrabies Falls National Park, it flows through a breath-taking granite canyon with a 240-meter (787 feet) drop.*

TOP *African Wild Dogs are highly endangered species. Their numbers are estimated at being merely 3000 to 5000 animals with approximately 750 of them living in Botswana. Southern Africa is one of their last retreats.*
RIGHT *African Wild Dogs are considered the best hunters amongst the mammals. Nine out of ten hunts are successful. They devour their prey hurriedly, as the stronger lions and hyenas are often quick to arrive at the scene. Young, pregnant or sick animals who cannot take part in the hunt receive their share of the food, too. African Wild Dogs voluntarily regurgitate the meat until the prey has been divided up equally amongst all the members of the pack.*

EMERALD IN THE SAND
THE OKAVANGO DELTA

SLOWLY WE GLIDE ACROSS THE CLEAR WATER, almost without making a sound. Schools of small silvery fish dart into the underwater forest, seeking cover. A formation of Nile geese flies overhead, honking loudly. Jacanas delicately balance on fields of water lilies in bloom. Hundreds of dragonflies dance in the sun in the wide reed beds. With a loud snort, hippos regularly emerge from the water, coming up for air. We deeply inhale the aromatic scent of wild sage. Almost miraculously, we shed the European hectic pace and start to relax, while we allow ourselves to be guided through the paradisiacal landscape of the Okavango Delta in a mokoro.

The mokoro, a narrow dugout canoe with a flat hull, can even be maneuvered quite easily through vegetated swamps. A poler pushes the wobbly boat along with a long wooden pole. The Bayei invented this type of boat when they settled in the Okavango Delta in the 18th century as anglers, hunters and gatherers. Traditionally mokoros are made of the hard, tough wood from the Jackalberry tree. Nowadays however, to preserve the trees, fiberglass is used to build the boats for the tourists.

When dusk falls, Shaku, our guide, heads back to our camp. He needs to concentrate, always keeping an eye out for the hippos. These huge creatures are a little jumpy and attack if you come too close. In the evening light, a choir of frogs begins to get ever louder. Nevertheless, we can still distinctly hear a sound much like the tinkle of a glass bell. It is the call of the Tiny Reed Frog, which is not even a centimeter (0.40 inches) long. It is a magnificent little red and white creature, sitting on the stems of the rushes. In the midday heat, the colors of this frog fade so that its now lighter surface can reflect the sunlight better. Still, what with being this much exposed, it is a miracle how this tiny amphibian does not dry out!

Early next morning we take the mokoro to a bird colony. Safe from predators, tens of thousands of birds breed on small islands, in the branches of water figs. Marabou Storks and Painted Storks try to seduce their partners by clattering their bills noisily. The efforts of some have obviously been rewarded – some females are already sitting on their eggs. The young pelicans have hatched. African Openbill Storks, ibises and various heron species arrive in large flocks to commence their courtship dance here.

See page 168

A hippo in the Okavango Delta, watching the goings-on at the riverbank, with interest.

Two young elephant bulls start fighting playfully while crossing the Khwai. Elephants are good swimmers. They submerge almost completely, using their trunk as a snorkel.

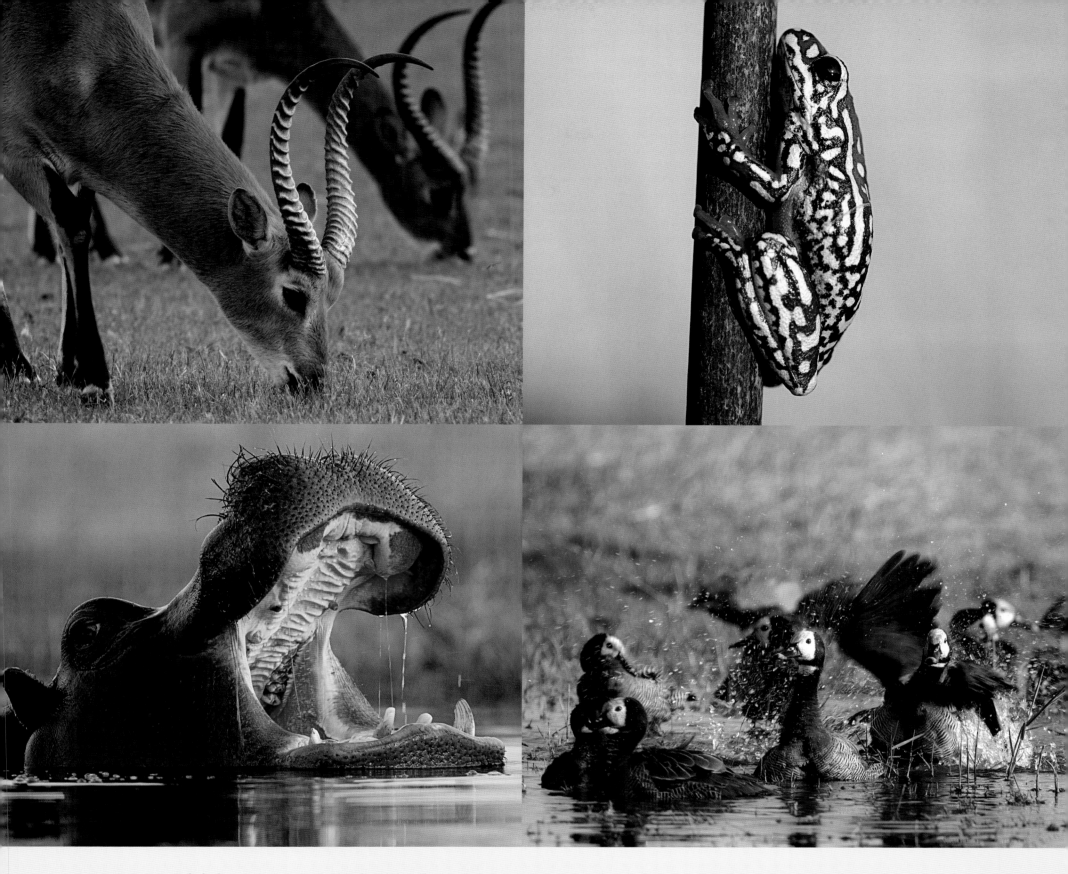

TOP LEFT *Male lechwes grazing on the banks of the Okavango. Close to the water, they have to keep an eye out for crocodiles.*
TOP RIGHT *The amazing colors of the Tiny Reed Frog fade during midday to better reflect the sunlight so it does not desiccate.*

BOTTOM LEFT *After lazy hours in the heat of the day, the young hippo awakens to new life in the evening with a big yawn.*
BOTTOM RIGHT *During the evening bath of the White-faced Whistling Ducks in the Khwai, the spraying water drops glisten.*

The Great Egret taking off is reminiscent of a ballerina. The bright green skin around its eyes indicates that he is ready to breed. Together with many other water birds, the Great Egrets have two main breeding areas in the Okavango Delta. They have a world-wide distribution and are found in Europe too, where they were almost completely eradicated at the beginning of the 20th century. At the time, their long feathers, which they grow in the breeding season, were highly prized for the women's fashion.

More than 450 species of bird live in the Okavango Delta. The breeding colonies of the water birds are amongst the most spectacular worldwide. Together with its unique flora and its extraordinary diversity of fish, insects, amphibians and large animals, the birds make the Okavango Delta one of the most species-rich regions on Earth.

On traveling through this paradise of swamps, lagoons and water channels, it is almost impossible to imagine that we are right in the middle of the barren Kalahari. The Okavango and the rain take turns in supplying the swamp area with water. In the winter, when the lack of rain dries out all life, the Okavango flushes the Delta with water from the mountains of Angola, 1,800 kilometers (1,080 miles) away. Just when the Delta has swollen to a size of 25,000 square kilometers (9,652 square miles) in August, it starts to shrink

again. The water evaporates quickly. Only a small percentage seeps into the ground or reaches the small town of Maun at the bottom of the Delta. From November on, the rainy season supplies the Delta with fresh water again. This semi-annual dynamic creates a mosaic of permanently changing watercourses, reed beds, islands, sandbanks and plains that remain submerged for some of the year.

We fly to the northern part of the Delta, to Vumbura, by bush plane. Our guide, Obonje, picks us up at the airstrip with a four-wheel-drive and drives us to our luxury lodge. It is the end of winter and the seasonally flooded grass plains are dry. Still, we have to cross several water channels of almost a meter's depth. In swampy areas, lechwes jump off, splashing. A pride of lions, hiding in the high grass, is waiting for the approaching herd

The bird colonies in the Okavango Delta are amongst the most spectacular on Earth. In the Pom Pom region of the south-west tens of thousands of African Openbills, ibises, pelicans, storks and herons all breed at the same time on small islands. In the branches of the fig trees, surrounded by water, they are quite safe from predators.

of buffalo. Elephants use their incredible strength to shake nuts down from the palm trees. A group of baboons benefit from this operation. They quickly grab a few of the palm nuts and eat them at a safe distance from the elephants. Dramatic cloud formations, thunder and lightning introduce the first rains of spring. While the violent thunderstorm rages outside, we enjoy our dinner in the dry – in the comfort of our lovely lodge.

Luxury lodges such as Vumbura are typical for Botswana. To protect its ecologically valuable regions effectively, the country has opted for high price tourism and a limited numbers of visitors. Only 50,000 tourists are allowed into the Delta per year. Apart from very few cheaper deals, a day in the Okavango Delta generally costs somewhere between 400 and 1,350 dollars per person. The Okavango Community Trust, which represents the interests of the local village communities, holds the land use rights. They lease large areas of the Delta for money and workplaces at the lodges, but keep a say in nature conservation issues and tourism activities. This is how the government tries to prevent international investors from exploiting the natural resources of Botswana.

Next morning we discover leopard tracks near the lodge. Obonje follows them right across the island, weaving in and out of the trees. We join the hunt excitedly. For us, too, a leopard sighting is a very special experience on a safari. To no avail however, after two hours we give up, disappointed. Before we drive on, we look back one more time. Wait, something just moved in the branches of that tree! At last, we spot the well-camouflaged animal amongst the green leaves. The female leopard had been watching us from up there for quite some time. This is the real luxury in the Okavango Delta – the encounter with wild animals in a pristine environment.

The female leopard spent one and a half years raising, feeding and defending her cub on her own in Vumbura in the Okavango Delta. Now that the cub has learnt to hunt, it is prepared and ready for the life of a leopard.

TOP *Leopards are real loners. They mark their territory with sharply smelling urine and droppings to warn all others that this area is occupied. The females, too, defend their territory aggressively against rivals of the same sex. The territory of a female, though, usually overlaps with that of males. Only if a female leopard is ready to conceive will she temporarily tolerate a male by her side.*
RIGHT *Leopards spend the day in the scrub or in the branches of a tree. With their spotted coat, they are almost completely camouflaged.*

TOP ROW *The tracks of the large mammals cross the landscape of the Okavango Delta like spider webs. The best way to appreciate the mosaic of water canals, lagoons, small islands and flood plains is from aerial view.*

BOTTOM LEFT *Large buffalo herds migrate to the seasonally inundated floodplains when the floods from Angola let the water rise again in the middle of the dry season.*

BOTTOM RIGHT *Lechwes flee into knee-deep water when they sense danger. Here their broad hooves enable them to run faster than the large cats and hyenas.*

PAGE 176/177 *A group of hippos spend the hot day in the cool water.*

TOP *Like many other elephants this lonely bull has migrated into the Okavango Delta for the dry season. While the rest of the Kalahari suffers under the drought, the Delta has more than enough food and water during this time of the year.*

RIGHT *A herd of elephants crossing the swamps of the Okavango Delta looking for food. Elephants eat various water and swamp plants, including reeds, which only very few animals can digest. But there is nothing they love more than the nuts of the Makalani Palms.*

TOP *Every evening the herons fly to their roost for the night. Here, safe from predators, they spend the night with other birds.*

LEFT *After the floods from Angola have reached the Panhandle in the north of the Okavango Delta water arrives in the south; this takes five months. This is when the delta swells up to its maximum size – in the middle of the dry season.*

A STRONG TEAM
THE LIONS OF THE DUBA PLAINS

DEEP GROWLING EMANATES FROM THE SWAMP. Mud sprays up in the air. Nine lionesses aggressively fight over their prey. Each one of them tries to grab a bite. Whilst crossing a watercourse they managed to steal a lechwe from a crocodile. They immediately snatched this chance of easy prey. This is typical for lions who, like hyenas, do not snub carrion either. It is clear that this antelope is far too small for all of them. Hurriedly the lions try to satisfy their craving hunger. Their feast is curtailed by a mighty male lion who comes charging in, mane waving, throwing himself into their midst with loud roars. The females scatter, reluctantly leaving their meal to this pasha.

With over 200 kilos of body weight, male lions are too heavy to make good hunters. Thus, they leave the hunting to the females. Nonetheless, they must come first during the feed – this is their right as the stronger sex. The life of a dominant lion is only enviable on first sight, yet. Night after night, he has to patrol the boundaries of his territory, scaring rivals away with his loud roars and marking his territory with urine. Yet still competitors will challenge him again and again. He has to fight them and these fights are often a matter of life and death. Most males only manage to maintain their position of dominance for a period of two years. As demoted pashas they are doomed to live a lonely life, feeding on mice and hares. To maintain their dominance for longer, often up to four males team-up to share a pride. The lionesses do not like frequent changes in dominant males either. With every take-over by a new male, their cubs are in danger. The new males kill them to be able to produce their own young as quickly as possible. Only females without offspring can become pregnant. As long as they have cubs, hormones suppress their ability to conceive.

The pride of lions in the Duba Plains, in the North of the Okavango Delta, consists of two males and nine lionesses with their cubs. For over 10 years, the 15-year old "Duba Boys" have been the bosses. Former trophy hunting had wiped out any competitors right up to the end of the 1990's. Coupled with this, the watercourses and swamps of their territory made it hard for a competitor to enter it. Consequently, the Duba Boys are the undisputed rulers of Duba, despite their old age. The nights shudder with their roars, heard from up to eight kilometers (5 miles) away.

See page 188

The female lions of the Duba Plains in the Okavango Delta are not in the least bit afraid of water.
When hunting buffalo they often have to cross watercourses and swamps.

Two lionesses of the Duba Plains, protecting their cubs. They do not like their sisters coming too close, as other females in the pride quite regularly kill cubs. This is unusual behavior, as usually cubs in a pride are raised together by the females.

TOP LEFT *The roaring male lion of the Moremi Game Reserve can be heard over many kilometers. The aim of his blood-curdling roars is to frighten away any potential rivals that have an eye on his pride. Female lions roar too, to keep in touch with other members of the pride.*

TOP RIGHT *After a successful hunt, the fully fed lioness lolls lazily in the grass for hours.*

BOTTOM LEFT *The aged 15-year-old "Duba Boy" was injured in a fight with the young males of the neighboring pride. A male lion very rarely reaches this age in the wild. Most of them die aged 7 to 12.*

BOTTOM RIGHT *Lions normally sleep during the day and hunt by night. The lionesses of the Duba Plains, however, have specialized successfully in hunting buffalo during broad daylight.*

TOP ROW *The two Duba Boys stay close to their hunting lionesses. As soon as there efforts are rewarded, the Duba Boys claim the prey for themselves. Only a grown buffalo is enough of a meal for the entire pride.*

BOTTOM LEFT *Hungrily the lionesses watch the resting buffalo herd. They know that the buffalo will need to get up soon to graze. Only then does the hunt, which often takes hours, commence.*

BOTTOM RIGHT *Hurriedly, growling quietly, the hungry lionesses devour the small lechwe, which they stole from a crocodile. They fear that a dominant male will soon claim their prey.*

The lioness of Kgalagadi Transfrontier Park looks almost petite compared to the muscular animals of the Duba Plains. While the Duba lionesses have specialized in the physically strenuous hunt for buffalo, the lions of dry regions must often make do with small prey, such as mice and hares.

Lions usually hunt by night. Apart from the fact that their night vision is six times better then ours, their relatively small heart has a tough time in the heat, so they like to avoid it, preferring to spend the whole day dozing in the shade. But curiously, the heat does not seem to bother the lions of Duba. They have successfully specialized in hunting buffalo in broad daylight. Their hunting technique requires a lot of strength and endurance. Packed with muscles, with a weight of up to 170 kilos, they are the largest lionesses we have ever seen.

When the sun rises the next morning, we spot the pride of lions watching a herd of buffalo resting in the grass not even 100 meters (330 feet) away. The lionesses patiently lie in wait until the buffalo rise to graze. Then they trot closer in a semi circle trying to pick out a weaker animal or a straggler. This is no easy task, as the buffalo stay close together.

Individual lionesses charge at the herd to get them to move. A limping buffalo falls back slightly. Quick as lightning the lionesses attack, but the herd comes to the rescue at equal speed. The lionesses retreat, but are soon ready for their next attack. Such a hunt can take hours, but it usually ends successfully for the lions. They kill around 15 buffalo a month. For years, their large experience has spared them any fateful counter-attacks. However, this proved not to be the case for this pride of lions whose territory was adjacent to the buffalo. One lioness after another incurred fatal injuries.

The buffalo is still alive, looking at us while the lionesses are devouring it. It takes several long minutes for death to relieve him of his agony. This time there is enough meat for all. Still, all that remains the next day is skin and bones. Finally, hyenas and vultures polish off these last remains. Near the carcass, the lionesses laze in the shade, their

A lioness on heat remains a little aside the pride with a male. What looks like a romantic tête-á-tête is actually extremely exhausting. They copulate several times an hour for a whole week. Three and a half months later the lioness will give birth to two or three cubs in hiding.

189

bellies full. They are satiated and will not need to hunt for a couple of days. Then their hunger will drive them back to the buffalo again.

The lions of a pride not only hunt together, they also share the responsibility of raising their cubs. They often give birth to them shortly after one another. They not only suckle their own cubs, but also their nieces and nephews. Two lionesses, lying a little apart from the pride, are grooming their two six-month-old cubs, licking them tenderly. Their rough tongue gets rid of dirt and parasites. Following a cool shower of rain, the young ones start to fight playfully. The grown mothers join in and romp around with their cubs.

Although the lionesses of the Duba Plains give birth to anything between 15 and 22 cubs annually, the size of the pride has remained stable for years. Cub mortality is generally high with lions. But in the pride, the young ones do not only die a natural death. Repeatedly, the lionesses of the pride kill cubs. A possible reason could be to prevent incest, as the Duba Boys, after so many years, have started to mate with their daughters and granddaughters. Alternatively, they may be trying to ensure that the pride does not exceed a certain size, as the food resources would be insufficient to support more lions. We can only speculate about the reasons.

Despite all these ecological problems, the Duba Boys have still not lost their interest in sex. Licking her passionately, one of the males tries to stimulate a female. Soon the two of them will retreat and mate several times an hour; but the days of the two old lions are numbered. Four males are growing up in the neighboring pride. At present, they are still too young, but soon they will be strong enough to take over the pride of the old Duba Boys.

A young male lion and his mother lick each other whole-heartedly. This keeps their fur clean and strengthens their bond. Grown lions of a pride strengthen mutual trust by licking each other.

PAGE 192/193 *Herds of elephants in the floodplain of the Chobe River in Botswana.*

"Every morning in Africa, a gazelle
wakes up. It knows it must run faster
than the fastest lion or it will be killed.
Every morning a lion wakes up.
It knows it must outrun the slowest
gazelle or it will starve to death.
It doesn't matter whether you are a lion
or a gazelle; when the sun comes up,
you'd better be running."

HERB CAEN,
AMERICAN JOURNALIST
(1916–1997)

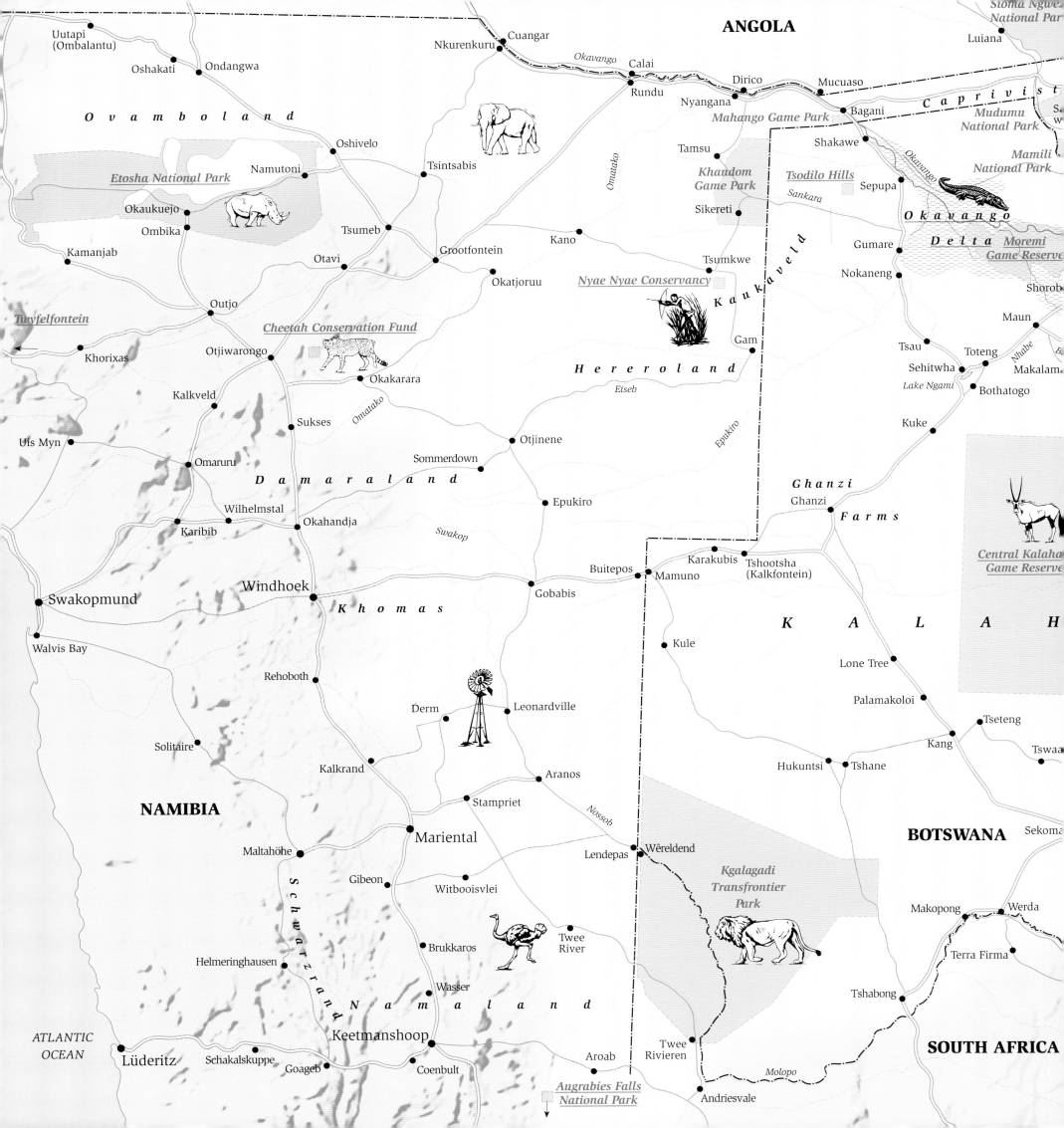

The KALAHARI extends from the north of South Africa over Botswana and Namibia to Zimbabwe, Zambia and Angola and into the Kongo. The light area on the map marks the core zone of the Kalahari in southern Africa where only the Zambezi, the Chobe and Okavango Rivers carry water all the year round. In other parts there is only enough water during the rain season. The countless fossil river beds have been dry for thousands of years. To this day there are only a few sealed roads in the Kalahari. Access is usually via gravel roads and sand tracks.

The book describes the pale regions of the Kalahari as illustrated on the map. The photographs and stories were collected from those protected areas and places which are underlined.

CREDITS AND IMPRINT

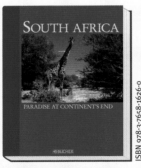

THE PHOTOGRAPHER

Lorenz Andreas Fischer, born in 1966 in Luzern/Switzerland, has had a passion for the natural environment since his childhood. After he was awarded a Masters Degree in Biology at the ETH in Zürich he began a professional career as an ecologist and high school teacher. Photography became an increasingly important part of his profession. Today he is a freelance photographer, specialising on the natural environment, alpine sports and travel. His main motivation for his work is fuelled by his fascination for the natural environment. His camera is a medium with which he can express his enthusiasm to an audience. He is the founder and director of the agency ALL-VISIONS, www.allvisions.ch

THE AUTHOR

Judith Burri was born in Lucerne, Switzerland, in 1965. She is a passionate traveller and has visited many of the most beautiful natural environments on Earth. Her fascination for nature incited her to study biology. Since her graduation with a Masters Degree she has been involved in environmental protection. Realising that media have a significant role to play in environmental protection, she also obtained a degree in the science of publishing. She uses descriptions of her personal experiences to foster public sensitivity about the uniqueness of the natural environment and the need for its protection.

ABOUT OUR PHOTOGRAPHS

The use of computer treatment and editing of the majority of the photographs in this book was kept within the confines of conventional and standard practices; to a degree that is permitted if entering major photographic competitions. Only a few of the photos are multiple exposures. Neither were elements from different photographs merged, nor photograph messages changed after the picture was taken. Except for the cheetahs at the Cheetah Conservation Fund, we exclusively took photographs of wild, free-running animals.

ACKNOWLEDGMENTS

This book was made possible through the exceptional support of a number of enthusiastic people. We would like to thank the following: Joachim Hellmuth and his team at C.J. Bucher Publishing in Munich, Germany, as well as the graphic artist Frank Duffek for his fantastic cooperation andhis faith in our book idea; Marcel Gehring and Christoph Huckele from Knecht Travels in Aarau, Switzerland, and Botswana Tourism, Namibia Tourism, Air Namibia, KEA Cars, Drifters Adventure Tours and Wilderness Safaris for their significant contributions towards our last three trips; Marco Rosenfelder and Hannes Felchlin from Nikon Switzerland and Mike Winter for his help with the remote-controlled camera; Fred and Onie Jacobs and all the people of the Bagatelle Kalahari Game Ranch in Mariental, their neighbors Peter, Judith and Kohus van der Westhuizen, Friedrich and Sieglinde Nauhaus from Gobabis as well as Karin und Mario Metzger for their cordial hospitality and all the useful information about agriculture in Namibia; Laurie Marker und her colleagues from the Cheetah Conserva-tion Fund (CCF) for their important work and for giving us valuable insight into cheetah conservation. – Thanks also to Graham Mc Culloch, the flamingo researcher from Sowa, for his cooperation; to Tjou, Bessa, /'Khaitieb, their families and the team of Intu Afrika as well as N/aici Kaqece and the people of Makuri Village for our time together living the life of the bushmen. – To George Tembo, Obonje Kamela and James Piseru, the guides of Wilderness Safaris who will never be forgotten, the staff of Jacana Camp, Duba Plains and Vumbura Plains and Shaku Otora of Drifters Adventure Tours in the Pom Pom Camp for some exceptional experiences and photographic opportunities in the Okavango Delta; thanks to Super Sande and the crew of Jack's Camp in the Makgadikgadi Pan for the stimulating discussions and the encounters with meerkats and brown hyenas; to Sandra and Jeromy Dacey and their successor Eric Botha of Drifters Camp Maun for their friendship and work on our base in Botswana; to Daniela Franziscus, Daniela Burkart, Patrick Schaller and Lorenz Fischer for a first critical review of the texts. – We would also like to thank Marlis and Josef Burri and Irma und Lorenz Fischer as well as our parents for always providing us with advice and support and for innumerable cozy evenings sitting around the kitchen table.

Finally, we would like to express our very special gratitude to the people of the Kalahari who are willing to protect large areas of wilderness so that wild Africa can continue to pulsate for future generations. As part of the Kalahari Project a multimedia show was also created. For more information, please visit the following website: www.kalahari-show.ch

C.J. Bucher Publishing,
Innsbrucker Ring, 81673 Munich,
Germany;
lektorat@bucher-publishing.com

Product management of the German edition: Joachim Hellmuth
Product management of the English edition: Dr. Birgit Kneip
Design: Frank Duffek, Munich, Germany
Translation: Jenny Baer, Vienna, Austria
Proofreading: Brian Leonard, Bad Goisern, Austria
Production: Thomas Fischer
Technical Production: Repro Ludwig, Zell am See, Austria
Printed in Italy by Printer Trento